The Good, Green Gold of Spring

A Conservation Sociology of the Island
Marble Butterfly

by

Jon Dahlem

Bellevue University

**Critical Perspectives on
Social Science**

VERNON PRESS

www.vernonpress.com

In the Americas:
Vernon Press
1000 N West Street, Suite 1200
Wilmington, Delaware, 19801
United States

In the rest of the world:
Vernon Press
C/Sancti Espiritu 17,
Malaga, 29006
Spain

Series in Critical Perspectives on Social Science

Library of Congress Control Number: 2022945913

ISBN: 978-1-64889-703-0

Also available: 978-1-64889-523-4 [Hardback]; 978-1-64889-550-0 [PDF, E-Book]

Cover design by Vernon Press. Cover image by Jon Dahlem. Island Marble Butterfly on Field Mustard.

Table of Contents

List of Figures

List of Tables

For Gimli.

Acknowledgements

I thank the Island Marble conservationists whose interviews made this project possible for their thought and insight. Thanks especially to the National Park Service for their kindness and assistance in the early stages.

Thanks to those who read and suggested revisions to the manuscript, especially Jennifer Sherman, Erik Johnson, and Jessica Goldberger. Thanks to those who read and provided comment on the book, especially Pierce Greenberg, Robert Fletcher, Oliver Pergams, and Jordan Fox Besek.

Thanks to friends and colleagues for their support throughout the project, especially Spencer Dickey, Dana Dickey, Kasey Cranfill, Kyle Knowles, Kyle Rakowski, and Aleksey Reshetnikov. Thanks to my family, the Theils, Dahlems, Dzialos, and Kings.

Thanks to Mabel for assistance in typing the manuscript.

Thanks to Liz Dahlem, who inspired, encouraged, edited, advised, and in all other ways made this book possible.

Thanks to the forests of Ohio and their inhabitants.

Chapter 1

Introduction

Commuting between the dry, early summer of eastern Washington's foothills and the perpetually rain-shadowed world of the San Juan Islands, there has not been a rainfall heavy enough to wash away the car's thickening coat of dead insects. Some might call it an unintended consequence, a bit of irony, or maybe a reason to hose down the car, but to an environmental sociologist, this is data. Here is some small evidence of a metabolic rift between planetary ecology and the machinations of human society. Whatever we breathe out, the natural environment breathes in. And on the road from Pullman to Friday Harbor, there is much more data: the Palouse's rolling, lunar hills mark the sacrifice of a state's greater ecosystem in the name of high-yield wheat production; near Washtucna, some small stands of wild regrowth cling to little rivers, gathering places for magpies and crows; through Ellensburg, drivers respectfully pass around two dead dogs discarded in the highway, frozen with rigor mortis; then cows, hundreds, packed in their pens; Snoqualmie Pass guides me through the Cascades, where steep, wooded slopes defy the economic rationality of saws; an hour of traffic keeps me slowly burning gasoline through the Emerald City's plant-decorated cement sprawl; Skagit County's more than ninety varieties of crop are an agricultural atlas along the roadside; and when the ferry pushes off from Anacortes, 55 dollars have bought me the privilege of leaving it all behind for the floating natural paradise of the San Juan Islands. I stand near the prow alone, watching cormorants in flight emerge and vanish through a thick mist, whistling to myself something low, tuneless, and melancholy, daydreaming of the orca songs faintly shivering through the cold, dark water below.

I am here searching for data that will help me understand the environmental sociology of the severely threatened Island Marble Butterfly. Over months of research, I will formally interview or casually chat with dozens of people involved with Island Marble conservation, and most will ask me, "Why the Island Marble?" In a betrayal of science, I tell them all that I am following intuition. In a roundabout way, I pose the question back to them: What motivates you to work on butterfly conservation? When did you start trying to save an insect from extinction, and when will you stop? What does the butterfly need from humans in order to thrive? What does the butterfly mean to you? In reply, I hear stories of hope, of fear, of duty, of the pursuit of knowledge, of healing, of despair, of balance, of anger, of pride, and of purpose. So much rests on the butterfly, inscribed on the species like scrimshaw. Like so many other species, I learned that the Island Marble is situated within the broken link between humanity and ecology. Everywhere, the socioenvironmental rift propelling this butterfly toward extinction and the remedial labor of its human allies are manifest in town, in research, in wild spaces, in art, and in so much more. Standing in the coastal prairie of American Camp, San Juan Island, WA, among the last of the Island Marble Butterflies in flight, watching the last of the southern resident orcas pass by offshore, I learn that what has led me here is not intuition at all. It is data.

This book presents original environmental sociological research based on a dissertation pertaining to social aspects of species conservation in the context of the Island Marble Butterfly (IMB) native to San Juan County, WA. The manuscript is composed for environmental sociological audiences first, general sociological audiences second, and general conservation science audiences third. Each section of the book contains language indicating which audience will find the section most readable and useful. Use of classical and contemporary sociological theory, research, and jargon, prominent use of external citations, and implicit use of a social constructivist perspective will clarify the manuscript's purpose to some readers while obscuring it for others. As such, I ask that non-sociological readers indulge me the adoption of a conditional curiosity for the sociological, and I ask that sociological readers indulge me occasional momentary pursuits of trans-disciplinary or persuasive prose. To this last point, I will clarify immediately that this manuscript is a product of both scientific research and environmental advocacy. This dual impetus is realized without conflict through a coupling of objectivity in empirical research and rationality in subsequent policy and action recommendation. Readers will recall that this research occurs in the socio-biophysical context of a rapid, global, anthropogenic ecological transformation amounting to a calculus of astonishing danger to known ecology and humanity.

In this light, this work puts forward three substantive chapters of environmental sociological research concerning human activities toward IMB conservation, as well as a chapter outlining existing theory and research on the social components of species conservation. Extinction and conservation are a small part of a greater environmental calamity and effort to abate it, and the IMB is a smaller part still. We will come to understand the breadth of human society's intersection with the natural environment through coming to understand the intersections' component parts. In particular, this research will put forward localized findings and theory to help understand why— despite scientific consensus and the prevalence of an urgent pro-environmental ethic—environmental calamity (including rapid biodiversity loss) progresses without meaningful human address. I describe a "conservation sociology" as well, not as a novel subdiscipline but rather a rally for sociologists to further study the phenomenon of species extinction and the social forces at work in species conservation. Unlike a "sociology of conservation," the conservation sociology described in this book (Chapter Two) seeks to develop sociological research that directly contributes to efforts to conserve biodiversity. In the process, I render as much as possible the sociological realities of the IMB's case: its history, discourse, social significance both local and global, and its embeddedness in broader social systems. I endeavor to tether these findings to existing sociological theory and research, to add to the construction of relevant theory, and to present findings that may inform future research. In sum, readers will find this manuscript a resource for understanding the social world of the IMB, as well as understanding the sociology of species conservation and portions of environmental sociology writ large.

This book consists of six chapters: three substantive article-length research reports, one literature and theory review, an introduction, and a conclusion. The literature and theory review synthesizes existing literature from environmental sociology, conservation biology, and other analogous disciplines, therein defining, positioning, and offering recommendations for a conservation sociology. Each substantive chapter addresses a distinct topic (meaning, power, and time) and presents a different contribution of conservation sociology to conservation science and action (empirical description, theory, and application, respectively). These chapters pose and respond to research questions such as: How are knowledge and meaning produced among stakeholders of IMB conservation? What is the function of social power in IMB conservation, and how do stakeholders perceive power? How do reckonings of social and biophysical time manifest in IMB conservation, how do these disparate reckonings relate to obstacles to conservation goals, and how can conservation sociology help conservation collaborations overcome such obstacles? The result is a set of disparate but related conclusions and a complex, multi-faceted discussion of the details of the IMB's case, the collaborations and contestations among actors therein, and the embeddedness of this case within a broader social context. In brief terms, the project finds that power and control of knowledge and action both among IMB stakeholders and between the conservation collaboration and its broader political-economic context render IMB conservation through local and global social systems, a product not only of science but of social forces. In particular, meaning and knowledge are rendered through a process of contestation among IMB stakeholders; power is invested in and divested from IMB conservation work by the ideological and material machinations of a capitalist political-economic context; and temporal obstacles to IMB conservation vary in recognition and treatment as they take sociocultural, biophysical, or socio-biophysical forms. These core findings are the foundation for the manuscript's broader contribution: the description, justification, and demonstration of a conservation sociology.

This introduction proceeds by first presenting general information regarding the species at hand as well as its conservation history. Then, the methodology of the research project is detailed, followed by an overview of the book. This introduction is intended for all audiences, containing generally accessible explanations of the butterfly's conditions as well as explaining the general thought underlying sociological research methods.

Island Marble Butterfly Conservation

The Butterfly

Figure 1.1. Island Marble Butterfly on Field Mustard

Euchloe ausonides insulanus perches on *Brassica rapa* (Photo: Jon Dahlem)

Euchloe ausonides insulana, or Island Marble Butterflies (IMBs), are the small green, white, black, and yellow butterflies of the Pieridae family that are native to the San Juan Islands in northwestern Washington state. Thought extinct since their last recorded sighting in 1908,[1] IMBs were rediscovered in

---

[1] It is worth noting that the 1908 sightings were limited to nearby British Columbia, Canada. The Canadian Species at Risk Act (SARA) listed the butterfly as extirpated in 2000, later re-confirming this status in 2010.

1998 by butterfly ecologist John Fleckenstein (Fleckenstein and Potter 1999; Guppy and Shepard 2001). In conjunction with the Washington Department of Fish and Wildlife (WDFW), including especially conservation biologist Ann Potter, Fleckenstein initially captured two small IMBs as part of a survey of prairie butterfly species in and around the San Juan Islands. The captured specimens were matched with the 1908 findings, and though at that moment the butterfly was indeed "rediscovered," the subsequent taxonomic designation and naming of the butterfly constituted its first real description and therefore "discovery," in the scientific sense.

When discovered, the IMB's numbers were thought to be in the low thousands, organized in several small groupings scattered across San Juan Island, Lopez Island, and perhaps beyond (Miskelly 2000, 2005; Miskelly and Fleckenstein 2007; Miskelly and Potter 2009; Hanson et al. 2009). From the years of 1998 to roughly 2014, IMBs are thought to have contracted back into a single population inhabiting American Camp, a peninsular National Historical Park located on the south shore of San Juan Island (Hanson et al. 2010; Potter et al. 2011; San Juan Preservation Trust 2018). Several highly local extirpation events are commonly believed among IMB conservationists to have contributed to this retraction, including losses of habitat on nearby Lopez Island due to human land use such as soil disturbance and lawn mowing. Approximately simultaneously, IMB sightings diminished at the nearby limestone quarry on San Juan Island. Further theories and competing notions of why the IMB ultimately retracted are explored in the manuscript's substantive chapters, but in historically certain terms, what is collectively held true is that as of 2018, the time of this research, the IMB meaningfully persisted only within American Camp.

American Camp and its companion park, English Camp, were established as National Historic Landmarks in 1961, due to their role in an 1859 Cold War incident between the United States and Great Britain known as The Pig War.[2] American Camp is a small park, consisting of a visitor's center, lighthouse, interspersed woodlands, roads, footpaths, sloping coastal prairies, shallow dunes, small lagoons, and beaches covered in little rocks and large water-smoothed logs. A great portion of the prairie is short grass, mowed by the rabbits making a home in the park. In the afternoons, a small crowd gathers with cameras to photograph foxes, who generally ignore the close human presence and roam the prairie in the open. If one is lucky, southern resident killer whales (SRKWs) can be seen swimming far off of the beach, whale-watching tours often in tow. While some of the high grass in which the IMB makes its home is fenced off by the local National Park Service (NPS), much of

---

[2] For a historical account of fascinating events of The Pig War, see Kaufman (2004).

it is not, and if one is endeavoring to spot an IMB, the general method is to stand in the prairie until you see a small white butterfly take flight, try to approach it before it flutters beyond reach, and hope that when you are close enough, you do not discover you have been pursuing the far more common Cabbage White. The park is a must-see for tourists, and for locals, it is a treasure.

Figure 1.2. American Camp

American Camp seen from the water (Photo: Jon Dahlem).

Figure 1.3. Foxes at American Camp

Photographers document foxes in the prairie at American Camp (Photo: Jon Dahlem).

IMBs have symbiotic relationships with several known host or feeding plants: primarily field mustard (*Brassica rapa*), tall tumble mustard

(*Sisymbrium altissimum*), and tall peppergrass (*Lepidium virginicum*), with known alternatives American searocket (*Cakile edentula*), small-flowered fiddleneck (*Amsinkia menziesii*), and field chickweed (*Cerastium arvense*) (National Park Service 2018; San Juan Preservation Trust 2018). Their core predators are thought to be wasps, swallows, spiders, snails, rabbits, and deer (through incidental herbivory) (ibid.). Due to habitat loss, predation, and non-native species proliferation, it is estimated that only several hundred IMBs remain, making it one of the most highly threatened butterfly species in North America (Guppy and Shepard 2001; Jordan et al. 2012; San Juan Preservation Trust 2018). Approximately half of this remaining population are annually reared in captivity by the local NPS.

Figure 1.4. Electric Fence at American Camp

An informational sign explains electric fencing to American Camp visitors
(Photo: Jon Dahlem).

In the IMB's lifecycle, its time as a butterfly is short-lived. IMBs begin as eggs, hatch into caterpillar larva that themselves undergo a series of severe and remarkable physical transformations through growth stages called instars, before constructing chrysalises in which to undertake metamorphosis, where they may remain upwards of 300 days of the year (Lambert 2011; Jordan et al. 2012; National Park Service 2018; San Juan Preservation Trust 2018). Metamorphosis and eclose from the chrysalis may be cued by environmental factors such as temperature. In the late spring through summer, IMBs emerge as butterflies, and for a period of a few days, the IMB mates and lays eggs, before dying (ibid.). Insect lifecycles such as that of the IMB present both conservation challenges and advantages because particular choke points may bottleneck populations and inhibit a growth rate that would advance rapidly in a hypothetical state of uninhibited reproduction (Shaffer 1981). Though the manuscript continues with very little further discussion of the biology and ecology of the IMB, for reasons such as understanding bottlenecking, predation, and butterfly-host plant interactions, such research must always be the cornerstone of conservation.

A Brief History of Island Marble Butterfly Conservation

Figure 1.5. Release of Captive-reared Butterfly

A biological technician with NPS carefully releases a captive-reared IMB
(Photo: Jon Dahlem).

After its rediscovery in 1998, the IMB became an object of interest for researchers, government agencies—particularly the Washington Department of Fish and Wildlife (WDFW), federal Fish and Wildlife Service (FWS), and National Park Service (NPS)—and local conservationists (Guppy and Shepard 2001; Hanson et al. 2010; Lambert 2011; San Juan Preservation Trust 2018). The WDFW funded studies that operated in conjunction with American Camp's NPS staff as well as local naturalists, especially including butterfly surveys (Hanson et al. 2009, 2010; Potter et al. 2011). These surveys generally adopted the "Pollard Walk" method, which essentially consists of scheduled walks through designated transects, during which surveyors count the butterflies they are able to see (Royer et al. 1998). In 2002, the Xerces Society for Invertebrate Conservation produced a petition to list the butterfly under the federal Endangered Species Act (ESA) (Black and Vaughan 2002). At the same time, local conservationists began investing in IMB well-being through citizen science participation, advocacy, and eventually captive rearing (National Park Service 2018). Local environmental advocacy organizations such as the San Juan Preservation Trust, San Juan County Land Bank, Friends of the San Juans, and Kwíaht became involved in collaborative projects. The San Juan Islands' communities, which have in part strong histories of collaboration with the natural sciences, responded to the IMB's resurrection with deliberate, collaborative, tangible stewardship (San Juan Preservation Trust 2018).

From 2004-2014, the NPS, WDFW, FWS, Bureau of Land Management (BLM), and several non-governmental organizations (NGOs) listed above collaborated on several research and conservation initiatives for the IMB, including formalized captive rearing at American Camp; funding scientific research on IMB populations, life-cycle, ecology, and behavior (Lambert 2011); prairie habitat restoration and preservation maintenance including controlled burns, soil disruption, and species control (grasses, brambles, rabbits, etc.); maintenance of human-butterfly relations in the form of education, fencing, and controlling recreational park usage; and efforts to control interspecies relationships, especially in the form of preventing deer herbivory using fencing (San Juan Preservation Trust 2018). In 2006, FWS declined to list the IMB as endangered, citing its use of multiple host plants as well as its existence in apparently disparate groupings on the islands (USFWS 2006). In the years immediately following, the IMB groups found outside of American Camp died off, as stakeholders were for a variety of reasons (explored in this book) unable to mobilize their conservation at those locations, instead focusing most efforts at the park. In 2008, a storm surge event is believed to have wiped out a significant portion of the lagoon-based IMB population at American Camp, further contributing to the species' genetic bottlenecking (Christensen 2017). Since its retraction to American Camp, the IMB has, as several interview participants put it, been persisting on "life support," almost certainly prevented from extinction by the direct intervention of a few dozen individuals.

Figure 1.6. Chrysalises in the American Camp Captive-rearing Lab

IMBs in chrysalises at the captive rearing lab in American Camp (Photo: Jon Dahlem)

The IMB conservation effort has experienced a great deal of turnover, changing in species leads at FWS, park superintendents with NPS, field technicians and interns with NPS who perform much of the IMB conservation labor, ecologists and entomologists employed by both universities and WDFW, and nearly a generation of San Juan Islanders. Still, some of those who were most closely involved with IMB conservation remain active in IMB advocacy. In 2012, the IMB was once again petitioned by the Xerces Society for listing (Jordan et al. 2012), and in 2017 the butterfly was approved to become a federally listed endangered species under the ESA. Efforts now exist to entice butterflies to populate beyond the park, headed by government agencies and NGOs alike, especially through a legal mechanic of the ESA which incentivizes landowners to contribute a small amount of property to developing butterfly habitat. Awareness of the IMB appears to be steadily growing among the community, especially as coverage by Oregon Public Broadcasting, KNKX Seattle Public Radio, Seattle's alternative newspaper *The Stranger*, and other media outlets cover its story as a compelling environmental narrative (Smith 2016; Flatt 2018; Pailthorp 2019). The IMB was officially proposed to be listed in April of 2018, and while several interviewed stakeholders expressed the expectation that a finalization of the listing would occur around April of 2019, the slow pace of bureaucracy prevented its listing until May 2020, at which point it finally became one of a small number of species federally listed since the 2016 U.S. presidential election. Now, with a growing body of public and professional support, two decades of research and conservation practice, and with the hope of an increasing number of suitable butterfly habitats, there is a notable spirit of hope among many IMB stakeholders. The IMB remains among the most severely threatened butterfly species in North America, but its careful protection, especially under the ESA, appears to give it a strong chance of persisting alongside its coastal prairie habitat, if not in a mode of growth and expansion, in a condition of isolated preservation among the strong conservationist and naturalist ethic of the people of San Juan Island and indeed the Pacific Northwest of the United States.

Methodology

The qualitative and ethnographic methodologies employed in this dissertation are greatly informed by Michael Burawoy's adaptation of the "Extended Case Method" (ECM) (1998, 2009). Burawoy's methodological project was to present a model of qualitative research that would demonstrate both high validity and the capacity to connect on-the-ground, deep social research to macro-sociological, structural theory in order to respond to a trend of positivistic critique of the fallibility of traditional qualitative methods in the social sciences (ibid.). He does this by eschewing positivism in favor of a self-reflexive relativism, freeing the researcher to acquire knowledge through a self-critical process of well-documented experience. This method relies on careful ethnographic notetaking, recorded in-depth interviews, rigorous maintenance of researcher integration with the studied community, and usually a considerable investment of time and participatory activity among the community studied. The result is a body of data that is in some ways particular to the researcher but is also made as internally valid as the human condition allows. Researchers can then analyze these social data to find evidence of social forces at work in the microcosm of the case at hand, applying and contributing to theories of social structure through study of a context embedded in wider social systems. Therefore, the local context is extended to the macro-sociological theory that is deductively applied to analysis.[3]

Additionally, this project's methodology is also greatly informed by contemporary qualitative sociological research, especially by Sherman's

---

[3] For Burawoy, the greater structural theory at play is a conflict-oriented, political-economic one. The scope of this book does not allow for a discussion of the base interrelatedness of political economy and ECM, but readers will note that the present research employs a similar perspective (Burawoy 1998).

contemporary application of ECM methods to interpreting the functions of social forces in rural American communities (2009), Norgaard's interdisciplinary theoretical approach to interpreting Norwegian climate change denial (2011), the qualitative analyses of scientific communities performed, especially by Frickel (2004) and Parker and Hackett (2012), and the multi-species ethnography put forward by Kirksey (2016). Readers familiar with these scholars will note their influence throughout, but the manuscript proceeds by singling Burawoy's prominent influence and describing the essential ECM applied.

To bring an ECM methodology to the case of IMB conservation, I endeavored to acquire a rich, experientially empirical understanding of the collaboration's scope, history, actions, key players and components, and core norms and values. To structure this methodological discussion, I will identify the key components of ECM, then explain how each component is realized in this project.[4] For the purpose of this organization, the central components of ECM might be said to be:

1.   Self-reflexive relativism;

2.   Ethnography, participant observation, and in-depth interviews;

3.   Deductive data analysis; and

4.   Theoretical connection between embedded and structural contexts.

To the first point, self-reflexive relativism is achieved through development of foundational research questions that do not require positivistic methods and a commitment to rendering internally valid data from the qualitative methods used. Positivistic research agendas might seek to identify associations between variables or isolate a variable association's causal mechanism. The research here instead asks questions about the depth and particularity of a single case, building complementary theory capable of describing the complex realities built around the foundational abstractions of variable associations. For example, Chapter Four will discuss in some detail the role of the political-economic context in contributing to the IMB's successful ESA listing, but these findings are not, say, interpreted as evidence in support of either hypothesis in a debate around the causes of biodiversity loss that test competing theories from environmental sociology, such as "Treadmill of Production" and "Ecological Modernization" (Hoffman 2004). Furthermore, self-reflexivity is employed both through rigorous attention to issues of validity (i.e., objectivity in observation; interviews without leading, misleading, or

---

[4] The language and organization of this section is largely my own and may vary from language used by Burawoy and others to describe ECM.

coercion; and careful parsing of facts from perspectives) and through reflection about researcher positionality, which will be evident throughout.

To the second point, data collection methods used here are modeled after the toolset standard to ECM, though they are adapted to the particular nature of the IMB conservation context. Interviews constitute the major data source, because it was possible to interview most individuals that had currently or at one point been members of the small IMB stakeholder group, and also because resource limitations made extensive participant observation and ethnography difficult. Still, significant ethnographic field research was conducted, including many trips to the San Juan Islands and around relevant sites in the Pacific Northwest. Extensive fieldnotes were taken from time spent in a variety of settings while participating in a variety of activities related to the butterfly and the local community. These multiple qualitative methods, discussed in more detail in subsections below, are supplemented by a modest amount of participant observation and archival research.

Data analysis relied on existing theory and research to derive coding and interpretation of patterns. Unlike a Grounded Theory (GT) method, in which the researcher conducts multiple rounds of data coding from a near assumption-less, *tabula rasa* position in order to inductively develop findings (Strauss and Corbin 1997; Glaser and Strauss 1999), ECM relies on researchers' expertise in structural theory and contemporary research to deduce patterns in the data that relate to contemporary discussions in relevant literature. The trade-off is such that one loses some exploratory freedom and gains a risk of super-imposing one's desired lens over data that is pointing in another direction. Still, ECM users benefit from an increased sense of research direction, the ability to relate findings meaningfully to structural theory, and the ability to facilitate participation in discussion with scholars conducting similar research. It is worth noting that this dichotomy is itself theoretical in some ways and that most research takes place somewhere between the two extremes, a reciprocal process of induction and deduction between new data and existing research. In this specific case, though the exploratory nature of the project did make GT an encouraging option, the salience of existing theory and research in informing the project's inception and development made ECM the more fitting choice.

Lastly, readers will note that each of the substantive chapters (Three, Four, and Five) will make significant attempts to relate the local embedded context of IMB conservation to broader structural socioenvironmental forces contemporaneously at work. In Chapter Four, for example, "power" is not understood as operating in isolation, but within the microcosm of IMB conservation by extension of broader social forces. Therefore, analysis relied on existing, established theory of social power and environmental politics. In Chapter Three, the development of IMB knowledge and meaning is interpreted through theory of the processes by which scientific knowledge more broadly is developed. Still, these analyses are not wholly deductive, nor are they confirmatory. Rather, case-specific, in-depth data yields an expansion of existing broader social theory to the embedded context of IMB conservation, and, as will be discussed in Chapter Six, perhaps to the embedded contexts of insect or invertebrate conservation more broadly.

Research Site: Island Marble Butterfly Conservation

Qualitative and ethnographic sociological research traditionally investigates communities that are bound by a shared spatial location. The community of IMB conservation stakeholders partially exhibits this spatiality, tethered in part to the butterfly's habitat, to the local communities of the San Juan Islands, and to the regional societies of Washington state, British Columbia, and the greater Pacific Northwest. Yet, the IMB stakeholder community is also significantly aspatial, taking form wherever individuals or organizations take on IMB conservation work. As such, while the IMB's condition is inseparable from the conditions of communities such as those of San Juan Island and Lopez Island, these communities were not the central focus of this book. Residents of San Juan County who were not otherwise identified as IMB stakeholders were not interviewed as *de facto* stakeholders. Instead, in addition to interviewing many stakeholders who were also San Juan Island residents, I travelled around the Pacific Northwest to meet verifiable stakeholders where they have made investments in IMB conservation from afar. Several interviews took place over the phone or by video messaging software, with participants located all over the United States and Canada. To be clear, the unit of analysis for this project is determined to be the IMB stakeholder group, with the term "stakeholder" being defined as having previous or current professional or voluntary engagement in IMB research, conservation, art, outreach, or any other IMB-related work.

Recruitment

In the social sciences, "studying up" refers to researching social groups more prestigious, resourceful, and powerful than one's own (Stich and Colyar 2015). Studying up is often difficult and therefore less common than "studying down," so there is an imperative shared among social scientists to avoid common non-random sampling errors across disparate studies. Researchers seeking "upward" access to prestigious communities often face obstacles in incentivizing participant recruitment, participant challenges to researcher authority, and higher research costs (Aguiar and Schneider 2012; Burrows 2016). Such upward study was the defining characteristic of this project's recruitment process. I confronted high ethnographic research costs in the San Juan Islands (e.g., lodging, food, gas, ferry fees), high standards of professionalism, complex scientific norms, caution, secrecy, and even occasional implicit or explicit contests against my credibility.

To address these challenges, the recruitment strategy employed measures designed to maintain methodological validity while overcoming social obstacles to upward access. Individuals were identified through rigorous online research and assembled into a spreadsheet that contained fields for associated email addresses and telephone numbers. The vast majority of individuals had publicly available contact information, and in the cases of those whose information was unavailable, I requested the information from their associates. Almost all recruitment took place via email. Each participant was sent a customized recruitment letter outlining my research, how I came to identify them as a potential participant, the purpose of the interview, and the topics it would cover. These recruitment letters relied heavily on an acquired proficiency with norms in science, conservation, and higher education. Many participants requested additional detail or communication before the interview took place, a process by which I performed the task of representing myself as intellectually and experientially capable of overseeing their interview. Additionally, as some participants engaged in IMB conservation from afar, their recruitment often required weeks of negotiation and planning, as well as willingness to schedule flexibly on all of our behalf. In total, only one individual refused an interview outright, and only seven individuals failed to respond to recruitment. The result is an excellent study in upward recruitment, by which almost all potential interview participants were recruited successfully through a rigorous process of customization, communication, and careful expenditure of available time and funds.

Interviews

The primary data source for this research consists of 31 in-depth, semi-structured interviews ranging from 40 to 90 minutes in length (averaging around 70 minutes), taking place over 8 months from April to December 2018. Most interviews took place in-person, with telephone and video messaging software used as an alternative. Interviews roughly followed a pre-designed, standardized interview guide, which was also personalized to each interview ahead of time (see Appendix A). Interviews were held in offices, in public spaces, and in cafés. Only one pair of individuals was interviewed, the rest being one-on-one. Interviews were recorded with a portable electronic audio recording device. Then, I transcribed audio files into text files using VLC Media Player and Microsoft Word. Privacy and security were protected through a process of assigning random numerical codes to interview files, keeping all audio and text files in a password protected laptop and external hard drive both held in a key-locked office or apartment, and finally by deleting audio files following transcription. Text files were then imported to NVivo qualitative software for analysis. Table 1.1 provides some detail about the composition of the interview participant group.[5]

Table 1.1. Characteristics of Interview Participant Group

Characteristic	# of participants exhibiting
Man	16
Woman	15
Government employee	18
NGO employee	8
Professional scientist	22
San Juan Islands resident	13

In general, interviews followed standard procedure for the semi-structured, in-depth style typical to ECM. Participants were presented with a Confidentiality Agreement approved by Washington State University's Institutional Review Board ahead of the interview and were given time to ask questions regarding confidentiality or the interview. The interviews themselves loosely followed the interview guide but were always personalized to participants' experience. Impromptu follow-up questions were commonly used to give participants time to pursue topics of interest and import to them, as well as to give the interviews a mutually engaging, listening-oriented quality. Precautions were taken to avoid leading participants, corrupting data with researcher influence, or corrupting data with abuses of confidentiality. The result is a set of interviews that exhibit strong internal validity and high data quality. Moreover, these 31 interviews represent the most comprehensive account of IMB conservation, science, and history existing anywhere.

The 31 interviews amassed here represent a quantity that is below the typical standard for qualitative sociological research, and so it is necessary to justify the sample size with explicit reckoning of the issue of saturation here. I

---

[5] Note: Characteristics pertain to when the participant was engaged in IMB-related work. For example, someone who now works for an NGO but worked with the IMB as a government employee is included in the Government Employee category.

believe my interview data gathering reached a point of theoretical saturation for a number of reasons. Firstly, it is important to iterate that available interviews were not left on the table, and that all identified potential participants who did not eventually sit for an interview were contacted at least once in request to do so (and most more than once). Secondly, the community of IMB stakeholders is quite small, and indeed the sample of 31 represents to my estimation a high majority of those experts, professionals, and laypeople that have explicitly engaged in IMB conservation work. Thirdly, interviews were rarely under an hour long and only included core IMB stakeholders as participants, resulting in a body of interview data that is almost entirely relevant, usable, and rich for analysis. Lastly, this level of representation is not of course required or standard in the present sort of qualitative study. Indeed, 31 is a low number for interviews (usually we seek 40-80), but in this specific case, it is actually a remarkable amount of coverage. As a researcher, I regret and miss the potential contributions of those omitted from interview data used in this study, but I am also compelled by the substantial participation and data contribution on behalf of the vast majority of IMB stakeholders who did participate to present this sociological analysis using the more than reasonable quantity of interview data achieved by the projects' undertaking.

In the chapters that present interview data, pseudonyms are associated with quotations. The use of pseudonyms is standard to qualitative sociological research. Pseudonyms help to conceal participants' identities, as well as to guide readers in distinguishing between participants and understanding how many participants are being cited in a given chapter. In rare cases, pseudonyms may be changed within the text in order to further conceal participants' identities.

Ethnography

Ethnography took place over six trips to San Juan Island, one trip to Lopez Island, and several further trips to relevant locations around the Pacific Northwest, including Seattle, Bellingham, Bellevue, Lacey, Anacortes, Mount Vernon, Everett, Olympia, Port Angeles, and La Conner, WA, as well as Portland, OR, and much else of the state of Washington. The six trips to the San Juan Islands amount to three weeks spent on-island. Careful notes were taken by hand in notebooks and electronically via laptop computer and cell phone. In the ECM style, these notes pertained to anything I deemed potentially relevant to research. All time on-island or on the road was spent in an ethnographic state, during which I recorded interpersonal anecdotes, conversations overheard among strangers, thoughts and feelings, ideas about research, notes on the local natural environment, and accounts of my excursions around towns and wild spaces. This is an intentionally broad definition of what is considered relevant data. The reality of species conservation in the Pacific Northwest is that it is diffuse. Conservationists will likely attest that their work requires a fair bit of travel, as few species are as limited in locality as the IMB, and as the IMB is far from the only species of interest to most conservationists, their work is rarely contained within any single locale. Therefore, an ethnography of IMB conservation is one partially detached from spatial boundaries, and it is this quality that I sought to explore within my means. The resultant ethnographic data is used here in a supplementary fashion, and the analyses are driven instead by interview data.

Archival Research

This research is also informed by a fair amount of secondary archival research. Such research is comprised of the collection and empirical examination of relevant texts, either through formal channels such as institutional records requests or by informally scouring electronic and physical data sources. Subsequently, collected archival data may be systematically analyzed using a variety of content analysis methods, or, as is the case here, data may be assimilated into a broader study as supplementary qualitative data. In this study, the data resultant from archival research are only occasionally presented, and this is done so in a non-systematic, supplementary fashion. As in other research that relies more heavily on interview and ethnographic data, this research uses archival data to gain insight into the textual manifestations of the research sample, to partially interpret the dominant discourse of the sample, and to verify interview participants' claims against consensus knowledge presented in these documents.

In particular, the archival documents analyzed in this study include but are not limited to: all peer-reviewed research articles pertaining to the IMB; all journalistic reports on the IMB and its conservation, as well as other threatened species native to the San Juan Islands; essays, books, artwork, and other texts composed by interview participants and other relevant actors; IMB ESA listing petitions, findings, and other documents formally related to the ESA, including the act itself; documents associated with non-profit organizations relevant to IMB conservation, including websites, action plans, annual reviews, statements, and many other varieties of text associated with non-profit conservation work; public texts associated with San Juan Island, Friday Harbor, Lopez Island, Anacortes, Seattle, and other communities related to IMB conservation, including local news articles, local writing and art, local online message boards and forums, physically-posted signage, and much more; websites, documents, and other texts produced by relevant governmental institutions; and more assorted texts relevant to IMB conservation. In sum, the archival research conducted here consists of three years of amassing and monitoring news, research, policy, and information regarding IMB conservation, the San Juan Islands' communities, and insect conservation broadly.

Data Analysis

Three rounds of ECM-inspired data coding of transcribed interviews, ethnographic fieldnotes, and archival materials led to the development of patterns of findings (Burawoy 1998; Sherman 2018). The first round took place most deductively. I followed a substantial series of notes regarding themes made before research began, during a literature review stage, and while data was collected, coding for particular trends that appeared salient or that could inform existing research dialogues. In the second round, further themes were developed in a free, modified GT style (Strauss and Corbin 1997), while existing themes were further revealed in layered coding schemes that made visible greater detail internal to each theme.[6] Finally, through a third round of coding, further layers were created to yield saturated detail within each coded theme. The result is that while other major themes than those discussed in Chapters Three, Four, and Five were rendered in analysis, what is put forth here are the three sets of findings that are most well supported by the data gathered, the most important to the IMB's context, and the most amenable to informing this scientific agenda, which is itself embedded in a context of contemporary environmental sociological and conservation biological dialogue regarding species conservation.

These analyses took place in NVivo Qualitative Software. NVivo is a popular tool among qualitative sociologists, as it uses computer power to make the mechanical processes of analysis such as organization, coding, storing, and searching far easier than traditional means of by-hand coding, while not sacrificing researcher freedom or manipulating intent. It is a complex, multi-use tool that lets researchers design and implement a variety of coding strategies (Bazeley and Richards 2000). In this case, it was selected for its security, its usefulness, and to replicate contemporary methodological standards of qualitative sociological research (ibid.).

---

[6] This coding process first admitted codes as they emerged, then narrowed to include only codes that proved most salient. The process revealed and included many codes that were not ultimately incorporated into analysis, including codes regarding gender, social class, disciplinary differences between ecology and biology, hope and despair, climate change, teamwork, expert/lay knowledge, political ideology, and more.

Limitations

Systematic sample exclusion is a limitation that is important to consider in this particular project. In this case, the rigor and extensiveness of interview recruitment allows for a fairly clear understanding of who is missing from the interview pool and why. Some suspected reasons for potential participants' non-response to recruitment or rejection of request may include: relative inexperience with the butterfly despite my having identified them as a stakeholder; concerns about talking to an outside researcher about sensitive conservation information; and unavailability. In each of these cases, substantial interviews were conducted with coworkers and collaborators of the un-interviewed to gain data that might be omitted by their absence. Only one organization was solicited without successful representation, the Bureau of Land Management, which in the San Juan Islands has very few employees and which, to my knowledge, has vocalized support for IMB conservation without taking any serious recent action.[7] Perhaps more concerning are omissions that reflect the parameters of what snowball sampling and other recruitment methods identified as key actors. For example, some participants maligned the IMB collaboration's failure to incorporate the perspectives of local indigenous tribes. Generally speaking, interviews with collaboration "outsiders" were invaluable to the research presented here, and it is probable that some outsiders who were unreachable or unmentioned may have provided further key insights. In sum, it is important to note that research here is capable of commenting on specifically the dominant discourse of IMB conservation as well as some, but likely not all, alternative perspectives.

The limited amount of participant observation employed here is associated with an inability to verify many participant accounts. Participation in annual collaborator meetings, for example, would undoubtedly have yielded useful data regarding cooperation and communication among organizational entities. To this limitation there is no real counterpoint; it is here simply accounted for in analysis the same way the absence of an array of would-be methods and data are accounted for: by ensuring research questions are appropriately matched with the data's potential. Provisions are taken where necessary to interpret first-hand accounts of participants as fallible and variable, in recognition that accounts are unverifiable without extensive participant observation and ethnographic work. As will be evident by the

---

[7] BLM owns land directly adjacent to American Camp. I do not know the extent to which this BLM outpost cultivates butterfly habitat, but no IMBs were said to exist there in 2018. Reasons provided by non-BLM actors included small staff size, pending legal permissions, and more. In any case, while BLM has been involved in IMB conservation, it was not found in this study to be a significant local actor at this time.

presentation of research questions and findings, care is taken to realistically parse the knowable from the unknowable as data are interpreted. Readers may find this description of methods and limitations thorough to the point of apology. However, the sentiment is not one of regret but of reflexivity. There are few factors in social research more important than realistic interpretation of what can and cannot be understood from the particular social data set being analyzed.

Overview

The work presented here was originally motivated by two broad questions: 1) What are the causes of and solutions to socio-political inertia toward species conservation? 2) What can a sociological perspective offer conservation science? To these ends, this research has succeeded in providing partial answers. Each subsequent chapter here considers a general subject area at the intersection of conservation and sociology, with an eye toward developing solutions to social conservation obstacles. The chapters each present unique sets of more narrow research questions to guide disparate (but related) research. Aggregated, these studies produce both general conclusions about the IMB's case and a thorough example of conservation sociology.

Chapter Two defines, justifies, and makes recommendations for the conservation sociology that is demonstrated by the substantive chapters. The chapter includes a literature review spanning environmental sociology, conservation biology, and similar disciplines; a comprehensive discussion of the distinguishing characteristics of conservation sociology; directions for methodological approaches and future research topics in conservation sociology; and an outline of the function of each substantive chapter in presenting conservation sociology's descriptive, theoretical, and applied use.

Chapter Three addresses knowledge and meaning-making, elaborating how conservation science is negotiated between groups in a broad cultural context. This research describes the contests and consensuses that result in dominant and marginalized understandings of the IMB, its circumstance, and its correct conservation actions. The chapter identifies three ideal-type groups of IMB stakeholders, defined by their shared values, norms, and beliefs. Using Boundary Theories (Gieryn 1983; Star and Griesemer 1989), the study describes and analyzes the dynamics between these groups. In sum, IMB knowledge, meaning, and practice is resultant from contests at social boundaries, rendering apparent in part the crucial role of external and internal social forces in the production of conservation science and work.

Chapter Four examines social power, comparing perceptions of facets of power to manifest realities. Using social theories of power, including Lukes's

"Dimensions of Power" (Lukes 1986), Weber's "Authority" (Spencer 1970), and Gramsci's "Hegemony" (Bates 1975), the analysis describes the distinctions between IMB stakeholders' perceptions of decision-making power and ideological power in IMB conservation work. The study concludes that IMB stakeholders tend to describe decision-making as being collective while it is often individual, and they also tend to neglect to describe the function of ideological power or the relevance of a political-economic context to their work. The chapter includes a discussion and conclusion that link the capitalist political-economic context in which the IMB is situated to aspects of its conservation practice. This work supports a growing thesis in the social studies of conservation, which suggests that the systematic neoliberalization of species conservation efforts serves to contain the capacity of conservation work to identify and address relevantly problematic components of political and economic systems (Igoe and Brockington 2007; Büscher et al. 2012; Büscher et al. 2014).

In Chapter Five, the role of social time is treated, especially as it pertains to obstacles to conservation effort success. The chapter employs a Bhaskarian critical realist ontology of environmental sociology to describe temporally related obstacles to IMB conservation—sociocultural, biophysical, and in-between—to prescribe solutions to these problems (Carolan 2005). The chapter concludes that individuals' social positions result in variable perceptions of "problems of time" in IMB conservation. Moreover, IMB stakeholders tend to describe and identify problems of time that are more sociocultural in nature but tend only to render prescriptions for related conservation action when the problems are more biophysical in nature than sociocultural.

Together, these topically diverse chapters all address one or more functions by which socio-political inertia is sustained toward addressing biodiversity loss and species conservation. Moreover, each chapter demonstrates a general, foundational contribution from sociology to conservation science, thus demonstrating conservation sociology's capacity for description, theory, and application. As such, Chapter Six is dedicated to synthesizing the substantive chapters' findings, reviewing the generalizability and practical application of the total research, and offering concluding thoughts on both IMB conservation and species conservation writ large. The general conclusion of the research project is that power and control over knowledge and action both among IMB stakeholders and between the conservation collaboration and its broader political-economic context render IMB conservation through local and global social systems, a product not only of science, but of social forces. In more specific terms, the IMB's case is suggested to express a quality uncommon among threatened animal species but relatively typical among contemporary conservation efforts: the state of its conservation is substantial in scope while remaining generally non-threatening to capitalist processes. Thus, IMB conservation, while nascent, is well-positioned to become integrated into the neoliberal culture and politics of local, state, and national conservation efforts (Büscher et al. 2012). Yet, increased representation and implementation of sociological perspectives on IMB conservation, in the form of conservation sociology, presents opportunities for meaningful address of the social obstacles that constrain IMB conservation work from addressing the root causes of its continued threatened status.

Thus, this book functions in a few ways. First, it contributes research to the sociological study of environmental problems by engaging in theoretical discussions among environmental sociologists on the topic of species conservation. Additionally, this research presents conservation scientists from a variety of disciplines with a discussion of how a sociological approach to conservation differs from other social scientific or biophysical scientific perspectives, as well as what such a perspective has to offer. Third, this work provides a kind of applied knowledge to IMB conservation. I offer this knowledge humbly and in acknowledgement both that conservation sociology, at the point of this authorship, is not yet legitimized in conservation circles and that even within the IMB's case, much further research could be done toward this particular end. Still, as any research on IMB populations or behaviors would be assimilated into conservation praxis, I submit that this research be admitted by stakeholders in their considerations of future collective action. Fourth and finally, I hope to make a meta-scientific argument for conservation sociology to be seriously pursued, citing not only its intrinsic value toward conservation knowledge-production and goals, but the structural necessity of applying a sociological perspective toward understanding and subsequently overcoming the major social obstacles to urgent pro-environmental action.

Chapter 2

Conservation Sociology:
What, Why, and How

The research presented in this book represents an example of what I will call here "conservation sociology." What is meant by this is that the work uses theory and methods from environmental sociology and applies them directly to the task of contributing knowledge that may help species conservation initiatives. There are many reasons why I believe this delineation to be warranted, and being that such work has not been substantially theorized, it is necessary to clearly define and explain how exactly this variety of work differs from what might be called "environmental sociology attending to species conservation." These reasons are explored in depth below. However, probably the greatest impetus for the delineation is simply that research from an explicitly sociological perspective that seeks to serve conservation goals is currently extremely rare. It is rare in spite of an urgent need for it to be common. By describing this work as conservation sociology, my desire is to mimic the very active language of "conservation biology" to draw attention to this need and provide a call by way of example of the kind of work that may achieve the two non-competing goals of 1) contributing to the development of theory and knowledge in environmental sociology and 2) explicitly seeking to create knowledge that will be useful to conservation actors.

Therefore, this chapter presents conservation sociology. The concept is defined, described, positioned among existing research, delineated from analogous sub-disciplines, prescribed methods for, and generally theorized. The chapter begins with a literature review that functions to relate perspectives in environmental sociology to conservation biology. Then, the resultant conservation sociology is rendered through detailed discussions of its basic assumptions, perspectives, approaches, and roles in interdisciplinary conservation collaborations. Finally, the chapter concludes with an overview of how each substantive chapter in this book demonstrates a use of conservation sociology to amount to an essential contribution of the project: the explicit naming, practicing, theorizing, and application of conservation sociology. The bulk of this chapter is intended for sociological audiences, and non-sociological audiences may consider jumping ahead either to the conclusion of this chapter, titled "Why Meaning, Power, and Time?" or to Chapter Three, which will pertain more directly to the specific case of the IMB.

What is Conservation Sociology?

Often described as the "Holocene extinction" or "sixth extinction," Earth has only seen precedent for the present rate of biodiversity loss at moments of extreme physical upheaval – mass volcanism, comet and meteor collision events, rapid sea level change, ocean acidification, and climate change. This time, the causes are human: habitat loss due to human land usage, chemical pollution, unsustainable fishing and hunting, introduction of invasive species, ocean acidification, and anthropogenic climate change (Wood et al. 2000). Much of the social scientific literature regarding biodiversity loss understandably concerns expected human impacts: increased rates of diseases; the loss of species whose anatomy may inspire pharmaceutical and technological development; drastic change or loss of natural spaces and their associated physical and mental health benefits, economic benefits, cultural significance and local usage; expected declines in food security; decreased access to traditional medicines; and more (Cardinale et al. 2012; Haines-Young and Potschin 2010). Yet, an interdisciplinary body of literature has also been growing for decades that advances theories of the interconnectedness of Earth's ecological and social systems, nesting issues such as species extinction in reciprocal processes of societal and environmental interdependence. Since the 1960s, formal academic research initiatives in environmental science, economics, anthropology, psychology, natural resource management, geography, forestry, and beyond have resulted in a diverse and rich body of research and theory on this topic. The present research concerns the specific divisions of environmental sociology and conservation biology. The thesis of the present synthesis is that the sociological perspective is currently in only limited use in the discipline of conservation biology, and that at the same time, biodiversity loss and its inverse phenomenon, species conservation, remain understudied topics in environmental sociology, despite compelling need for increased knowledge at this socioenvironmental nexus.

In the decades leading up to the new millennium, early American[1] environmental sociologists such as William Catton, Riley Dunlap, Eugene Rosa, and Frederick Buttel called for the growth of an environmental sociology designed to meet issues such as biodiversity loss with scientific research and

---

[1] It is important to clarify that this literature review primarily concerns the American context. American and European sociology, conservation, and indeed academics take place in quite distinct traditions. As much as possible, I have tried not to systematically omit relevant European research throughout the book. However, the present discussion may often be correctly read as a description of (American) conservation and (American) sociology, as in defining conservation sociology, I must limit the concepts to the American understandings of those two words.

well-informed policy recommendations. In 1999, Rosa wrote that "our greatest hope [...] lies with [...] an ecologically informed approach that offers hope for a second environmental science" (Rosa 1999:374). This "second environmental science" was to complement the first (i.e., biology, ecology, etc.) with a social perspective that attended to the messy interconnectedness—feedback loops and indirect, complex equations—of human and ecological systems. As an example of such research, Rosa cites Gary E. Machlis (Machlis 1992; Forester and Machlis 1996), who operationalized social and ecological variables associated with biodiversity and developed frameworks for interpreting the relationship between these variables. In particular, Machlis drew from ecological research to argue that human population growth, increased production and consumption, and a factor of technological efficiency were the root causes of species extinction, operating through processes of ecosystem exploitation such as hunting, resource extraction, land conversion, pollution, and climate change. This work sought to convert theory from the natural sciences to social theory, to use and be of use to natural scientists, and to lay foundation for environmental sociologists to occupy a position among the sciences (and indeed the public sphere) as irreplaceable experts in the interconnectedness of the human social and environmental worlds.

The research directive of sociologically interpreting social causes and consequences of biodiversity loss, particularly in the age of anthropogenic climate change, incited by Machlis, Rosa, and others, has not been effectively taken up by American environmental sociologists (though this is not to say that climate change, unequal exposure to pollution, and other environmental phenomena have not been rigorously studied). Consequently, an array of literature, mostly produced by natural scientists, has filled this lacuna for the purposes of the broader scientific community. While much of this work has produced the beginnings of what is here called a "conservation sociology," or a subsection of environmental sociology explicitly concerned with generating knowledge that will contribute to species conservation work, this subsection has yet to be formally described or realized in collective research. As it stands, sociological research in conservation biology is rarely taught or cited by environmental sociologists, and sociological research is at least rarely cited by conservation scientists. Environmental sociology is aptly stationed to begin assembling the jigsaw of existing research on the human causes of biodiversity loss and to take the lead in producing research that fills the many gaps in our understanding of this subject. It will be a complicated matter of environmental sociologists increasing their presence in the public sphere and their collaboration across the aisles of academia, as well as natural scientists abandoning an incoherent, contradictory treatment of the issue that subjugates the anti-positivistic vein of social scientific methodology while refusing to apply a truly empirical perspective to the social world (i.e., adopt rigorous sociological methodology). Collaboration between natural scientists and social scientists will lead to better science and policy regarding species extinction and conservation.

With this call for research delivered, it is important to recognize the contributions environmental sociologists have thus far made to the study of biodiversity loss. Hoffman operationalizes a neo-Malthusian theory of population growth, treadmill of production theory, ecological modernization theory, and world systems theory, using national characteristics that predict species endangerment to find support for ecological modernization and treadmill of production at varying levels of the world system as explanatory models of biodiversity loss (2004). Moreover, Shandra et al. find cross-national support for the theory of ecologically unequal exchange (2009, 2010), while McKinney et al. find that the structure of the global system contributes to biodiversity loss internationally (2010). Additional research has examined the relationship between environmental concern and concern with/knowledge of biodiversity loss (Hunter and Brehm 2003; Hunter and Rinner 2004). These authors recognize in their publications that this topic remains understudied, a theoretical gap addressed by Besek and York (2019), whose article assesses the current state of research on this topic from much the same position as this book, finding that contributions from environmental sociology represent compelling perspectives as well as limitations in the present understanding of a sociology of biodiversity loss and can be supplemented by perspectives across sociological subdisciplines. Taken together, this research has begun the important work of applying existing major environmental sociological theories to biodiversity loss. It is meaningful that quantitative research has verified that these theories are in part generalizable to this issue because it indicates that the research in this area need not start from scratch—environmental sociology (and sociology more broadly) is already in part methodologically and theoretically equipped to address the human causes of biodiversity loss.

However, future research must account for the limitations in past research design. In particular, biodiversity loss cannot be fully explained by simply treating it as a form of environmental degradation indistinguishable from deforestation, air pollution, and others. The theories and variables that have established explanatory power with regard to, say, national carbon emissions, cannot fully explain biodiversity loss. Quantitative models will gain explanatory power by addressing key ecological variables that explain and predict species diversity and population. This means that ESA registries and NGO threatened species lists are insufficient as dependent variables to fully comprehend this phenomenon, as they fail to measure species richness, diversity, and relative abundance. Future research must take into account specific ecosystems and the specific roles of species therein, becoming the "second environmental science" through incorporation of direct ecological research (Rosa 1999). Where quantitative methods can explore ecological variables, qualitative methods are necessary to explore ecological contexts in depth. Qualitative studies such as this one that interpret localized human causes and consequences of biodiversity loss can help to build theory and explore its application, as well as ground this research in a set of real causal mechanisms which can be glossed over by reductive analyses. For example, the present study will put forward partial explanations of IMB conservation outcomes that suggest social variables *may* hold more sway over conservation outcomes than ecological variables, but evidence for such an assertion would require statistical models capable of measuring and comparing the explanatory power of variables.

Lastly, it is important to recollect the contributions to the sociological study of species conservation made by social scientists and natural scientists alike (often in interdisciplinary cooperation). There is a body of literature among the social sciences beyond sociology that is extremely relevant and useful to conservation sociology broadly, particularly put forth by psychologists and economists who have long since named and described a "conservation psychology" (Saunders 2003) and a general "conservation social science" (Bennett et al. 2017). Below follows brief reviews of the contributions of conservation psychology, conservation economics, and conservation social science generally, with emphasis on the emergent study of the neoliberalization of species conservation.

Conservation psychology is the subfield of psychology that pertains explicitly to research motivated by the goal of further environmental sustainability (Saunders 2003). This research emphasizes the dual goals of uncovering the cognitive and behavioral processes that govern both caring for and acting on behalf of non-human species (ibid.). Scholars of conservation psychology ask questions like, what is the role of the discipline of psychology in realizing conservation goals (Clayton and Brook 2005)? Or, what is the nature and purview of the psychological components of conservation (Saunders and Myers 2003)? They apply psychological theory and methods to specific cases, considering such topics as how the human mind perceives and relates to animal groups such as insects (Simaika and Samways 2018), how human connections to wildlife motivate conservation behavior (Skibins and Powell 2013), the relationship between conservation and the human capacity for caring and compassion (Rabb and Saunders 2005; Bekoff 2013), and how decision-making in conservation occurs (Papworth 2017). The general contribution of this literature is a detailed analysis of how a conservation ethic comes to be adopted by individuals, how this ethic then translates into behavior, and how these processes may vary based on the species or ecosystem in question. This research is closely tied to yet distinct from the objectives of conservation sociology, and as with the broader disciplines of psychology and sociology, as they continue to develop there will likely be significant overlap and significant differences in perspective. In general, while social psychology tends to operate at the interdisciplinary nexus, general sociology is more concerned with what social things exist outside of the mind, while general psychology is more concerned with how the mind operates and relates to behavior.

Conservation economics generally concern the operations of conservation work within the capitalist economic system. The undergirding logic of conservation economics is that economic conditions determine species risk, that the costs of species protection are priorities in conservation decision-making, and that economic incentives are essential motivators of conservation behavior (Shogren et al. 1999). These studies analyze specific issues such as the economic viability of farming wildlife in order to diminish poaching (Damania and Bulte 2007), the costs and benefits of *ex situ* and *in situ* plant and animal conservation (Damania and Bulte 2001; Li and Pritchard 2009), and whether the social benefits of protecting species outweigh their private and public costs (Brown and Shogren 1998). Economics and sociology share foundational ideas and a prioritization of the material conditions of the social world. However, they tend to vary immensely in their conclusions. As will become apparent throughout this manuscript, the very economic system which economists of conservation tend to hold implicitly natural and immovable will be discussed in the light of its arbitrary nature among/underneath social systems, and indeed in places this system will be critiqued for its role in extinction and conservation.

Conservation social science, as it exists relatively untethered from any singular discipline's traditions and norms—as it commonly takes form when conditionally adopted by natural scientists, though it is not exclusively performed by that group—is concerned with removing the transdisciplinary barriers to social research in conservation (Fox et al. 2006), integrating social scientific methods such as qualitative methods in conservation research (Moon et al. 2016; Rust et al. 2017), and synthesizing the contributions of conservation psychology, economics, etc. (Bennett et al. 2017). There are a remarkable number of articles and essays, which are generally abstracted from research and tend to feature several co-authors from varying disciplines, that make explicit, meta-scientific calls for increased social scientific research in conservation work (Mascia et al. 2003; Sandbrook et al. 2013; Bennett et al. 2017; Teel et al. 2018). There has been a clear articulation of the necessity, desire, and performance of social research in conservation over the last twenty years. The present work participates in this growing body of research, very much in an attempt to answer these inclusive calls to scientific action.

Much of the project of conservation social science has been to identify problems with popular approaches and perspectives in conservation and to then offer solutions to these problems. For example, Berkes' recent work *Advanced Introduction to Communty-based Conservation* describes the inadequacy of contemporary conservation efforts, citing issues such as the poor record of curbing the acceleration of global biodiversity loss overall, the historical tendency of mainstream conservation not to account for the interrelatedness of natural and human social systems, the exclusion of indigenous perspectives and knowledge, and the perennial failure to reach international targets set by the Convention on Biological Diversity (CBD) (2021). Berkes ultimately offers a series of principles of "community-based conservation" as solutions: building on local cultures' varied stewardship traditions; recognizing the interrelatedness of biodiversity and cultural diversity; inviting indigenous communities into conservation governance partnerships and learning from indigenous knowledge sources; implementing broadly multi-level, participatory conservation governance; and more. This variety of scholarship performs the vital function of what sociologist Erik Olin Wright called "envisioning real utopias," of going beyond a critique of the contemporary political-economic system and its many designs of culture and social structure (including conservation theory and practice) and rather describing the alternative systems that could supplant them (2010).

Similarly, in *Biodiversity Conservation and Poverty Alleviation*, Roe et al. collect a comprehensive set of approaches from conservation scientists and activists to investigate the relationship between poverty and biodiversity loss, amounting to strong support for the thesis that human poverty is inextricably linked to biodiversity loss in a number of ways (2012). For example, unequal access to ecosystem services along lines of economic inequality is associated with ecosystem health (Turner et al. 2012); relationships between poverty and biodiversity loss vary by socioenvironmental context (Campbell and Townsley 2012; Mortimore 2012); and the solutions to poverty and biodiversity loss are interrelated in complex ways (Elliott and Sumba 2012; Leisher et al. 2012). These works are generally policy-oriented, and many of the suggestions made in the collection, drawn from the conclusions of specified research, may be considered if implemented quite politically and economically radical. As just one example, Wittmer et al. make recommendations such as the development a pro-ecological lobby, introduction of regulation to prevent policy and (economic) projects from unintentionally degrading ecosystem services essential to the poor, investment in ecosystem restoration, and policy toward general poverty reduction (2012). Thus, while no real overarching analysis emerges from the collection to implicate a singular extant political-economic structure that results in both poverty and biodiversity loss, the solutions proposed implicitly invite transformation of that system. This contribution is salient because this kind of strong policy recommendation nested within an analysis that maintains the invisibility of political-economic structures is mirrored in the general socioenvironmental conclusions of significant international conventions such as the CBD.

One interdisciplinary theoretical perspective to emerge from conservation social science that fits very well among prominent theories of environmental sociology and also ties together many of the ideas above is the theory of the neoliberalization of species conservation (Roth and Dressler 2012; Büscher et al. 2014; Fletcher 2012, 2014; Büscher and Fletcher 2020). This theory undergirds some of the essential conclusions of this book and is worth treating here. Just as social scientists of conservation may note and attend to the specific mechanics of a capitalist economic system in conservation and extinction outcomes, so must they attend to the broader extant, dominant political-economic ideology of the contemporary context, which is summarily theorized by some as neoliberalism. Neoliberalism refers to the ideas and rationale that free markets, free trade, private property, and the practices that consequently uphold these phenomena are the appropriate guide to achieving optimal human social outcomes (Harvey 2005). Scholars of neoliberal conservation conclude that contemporary conservation work, in its current form, participates in the neoliberal tradition of political and economic design, not threatening existing systems, but working to support them. Specifically, neoliberalized conservation takes the form of "introducing market mechanisms or market-like models of decision-making, privatisation, and commodification of conservation goods or services, monetisation and valuation, and a re-orientation to private sector financing" (Youdelis 2018: 257). These scholars study such topics as contextualizing international conservation efforts among international political and economic relations (Büscher 2010; Youdelis 2013), austerity among government organizations related to conservation (Youdelis 2018), the constraints scientists face as to what they can publish, say, and endorse (Turner 2013), and the exclusion of indigenous people from conservation work (Maclaren 2011; Youdelis 2016). This work constitutes by definition a theory of the sociology of conservation, capable of describing and predicting the social organization of conservation work as well as integrating these models with broader related theory, and it is thus adopted here in a reoccurring and basic fashion.

In response to this theory of conservations' neoliberalization, Büscher and Fletcher put forth in *The Conservation Revolution: Radical Ideas for Saving*

Nature Beyond the Anthropocene an alternative conservation paradigm capable of addressing root social, economic, and political obstacles to serious prevention of biodiversity loss (2020). The authors parse conservationism(s) along axes of capitalist/beyond-capitalist and observance or not of a nature/culture dichotomy. What they label "mainstream conservation" is that which is works within capitalism and perpetuates a dichotomy between nature and culture (i.e., a neoliberal model of conservation). What they label "convivial conservation" and subsequently argue for throughout the text is that which is beyond-capitalist and beyond the nature/culture dichotomy. Büscher and Fletcher adopt much of the language and concepts of sociology but identify their analysis with political ecology, approaching this topic from a broad, meta-disciplinary angle that considers the perspectives of popular texts in environmental media, social movements, and scientific/intellectual movements toward understanding where we are as conservationists, where we may be headed, and where we should be headed to achieve our shared objectives. Readers will detect through the following substantive chapters that this text takes place in the tradition of such a "convivial conservation."

The emergence of a conservation sociology, then, is gradual but eventual, and the present contribution of the author to expediting this process is less a unique intellectual contribution and more a concerted amplification of an emergent need for research on this topic. Indeed, the term "conservation sociology" has already been coined by Pergrams (2019), and others have implicitly or explicitly called for essentially the same imperative (Bennett et al. 2017). The issue is not that a conservation sociology does not yet exist, for indeed several researchers have already begun the work of constructing its foundations (Machlis 1992; Belsky 2002; Peterson et al. 2005, 2006; Hoban and Vernesi 2012; Peterson et al. 2013; Gustafsson et al. 2015; Nel et al. 2015; Bennett et al. 2017; Besek and York 2019; Pergrams 2019). Rather, the present call for a conservation sociology is motivated by an apparent need for this literature to become collected, self-integrated, communicated, given ample space, and established meaningfully within environmental sociology. Indeed, much of the work that is explicitly sociological or calling explicitly for future sociological contributions takes the form of letters and opinion editorials rather than research articles, and there is not yet a peer-reviewed academic journal dedicated to the sociology of biodiversity conservation (though there are analogous yet distinct journals such as *Conservation & Society*). It is largely the project of this book to make the point, by way of example through research, syntheses of literatures, and direct argumentation, that this establishment of conservation sociology within environmental sociology would be a valuable and effective collective action on behalf of its proponents.

Further on, this chapter tackles the significance of applying sociological theory and methods to conservation issues, as well as the more nuanced aspects of parsing sociology from other disciplines. Before and below, however, is a brief outline of the advantages of conservation sociology, in broad terms, to make this purpose plainer:

1. **Conservation sociology will offer new perspectives to conservation science.** Conservation science, or conservation biology, when it endeavors to study social things, as of yet prefers the psychological and economic perspectives over the sociological. This matters because sociology consists of fundamentally distinct conceptions of both what exists and what is to be studied. In particular, sociology emphasizes the role of institutions and other social structures, frequently considering these structures the central objects of analysis. The three substantive chapters here have demonstrated this by employing a kind of Weberian cultural materialism, which characterizes most contemporary sociology, by which the economic underpinnings of society are recognized yet understood as existing through negotiations of culture, power, and other social forces that lay atop and render through action the economic foundation. For example, while research in conservation biology speaks frequently of "species charisma," which is a psychological concept, a sociological perspective on the same concept demands further analysis, as cultural meanings vary by social context (time and place), and so "charisma" must be linked to culture and social structure beyond what our current grasp suggests. In the substantive chapters that follow, phenomena such as charisma are generally omitted as explanatory concepts in favor of more sociological explanations of conservation outcomes.

2. **Sociology often disrupts preconceived notions of society.** Sociologists know well that resting back on anecdotal knowledge of the social world is not the best analytic for understanding it. Yet, the anecdotal phenomenon is not uncommon among conservationists untrained in the social sciences who seek to make comment on important social components, even those who live and work by a code of empiricism. Humans share this tendency toward privileging the fallacious logic of anecdote, so human sociologists must constantly remind themselves to avoid speculation and to return to data, however difficult social data may be to come by. Conservation sociology is a framework that deliberately seeks to cease relying on personal reflection on anecdote when describing and explaining the social components of species conservation and to instead rely on

peer-reviewed, rigorously managed scientific research. Scientists and conservationists can and should hold our social scientific contributions to a high standard of empiricism.

3. **Sociology is a rigorous scientific discipline with rich theoretical and methodological traditions.** The scientific discipline of sociology is in its current form two centuries old, which is also roughly the age of modern biology. The amount of theory and research that exists therein is reflective of this long tradition. While the siloing of sociology in conjunction with its late entry into environmental discussions has apparently resulted in its even later formal entry into conservation science, this siloing has also cultivated a quite unique perspective. The book attempts to discuss this perspective throughout and does so again below. In the plainest terms, while sociological research by non-sociologists is not at all impossible, research performed by sociologists is particular in nature and has particular advantages.

Why "Conservation Sociology"?

The purpose of describing the present work as conservation sociology is not to attempt popularization of a neologism,[2] nor to imply conservation sociology is not already underway under other monikers (as discussed above, it very much is!), nor to promote a critique of conservation biology, conservation psychology, or other extra-sociological analogues. Rather, this description of conservation sociology is meant to give attention to a concept that demands further research. In describing the concept, what is meant is to accomplish what has been accomplished, for example, in the life sciences, as Foucault points out, with concepts such as "life" and "human nature" (Chomsky and Foucault 1971). For Foucault, it is unclear that these concepts can ever be permanently, concretely defined in the sense of concepts which have organizing roles, and it is unclear that this is their purpose. Similarly, conservation sociology, as a concept, is not meant as itself to be an instrument of analysis or description of reality. Rather, the concept serves "to designate, to delimit and to situate a certain type of scientific discourse" (ibid.). For this reason, it is practically nonsensical to attempt to present scientific proof of the existence of a conservation sociology or even the

---

[2] Indeed, to reiterate, this work does not coin "conservation sociology," as conservation biologists Drs. Oliver Pergams and Patricia Zaradic have done so on Pergrams' personal web page in a call for increased research in this area. However, as they are making a very general call for increased social scientific research, for all intents and purposes, the first formal definition of the term is appearing here (Pergrams 2019).

impetus for one, including the existence of what is called here many times "the social components of species conservation." While these components will have measurable individual existences, it will be impossible to draw, in observable reality, parameters of the total concept (i.e., certainty of what is or is not a social component of species conservation), as it is a discursive construct rather than a concept capable of concrete definition through empirical research (e.g., the periodic table of elements). These concepts' description is here instead *grounded in practical necessity*. It is a meta-scientific annunciation of needed research, more akin to a "literature gap," "call for papers," or scientific discipline than a concept that is itself testable. I make this distinction to avoid confusion over the genesis of the definition I provide. I have not empirically sought to explicate the concept's definition; I have authored the concept's definition to serve a purpose based in scientific and environmental advocacy. In addition, readers will not find that research into the IMB has in and of itself explicitly generated the necessity to frame the research in this way. Rather, it is necessitated by the need to contextualize my work in relation to existing research in environmental sociology.

Briefly, to treat the semantic issue of developing a "conservation sociology," it is worth noting that the term out of context is nonsensical, but in context, there is no more appropriate term. "Conservation" refers by definition to the prevention of the waste of anything. Indeed, many things other than biodiversity can be conserved: water, land, minerals, food, funds, energy, etc. "Conservation biology," however, which is the study of the conservation of life, has resulted in a connotative association of the word "conservation" with the conservation of non-human life, especially animals, plants, fungi, and other species that are considered wildlife. For this reason, the term "conservancy," or a place where things are conserved, is reserved primarily for biological conservation. Moreover, "conservation" as an ethic is defined explicitly as wildlife conservation. There is no word in English more apt to describe the prevention of loss of non-human living things than "conservation." For this reason, this book names the concept at hand conservation sociology, which is here defined as environmental sociological research that seeks to contribute to species conservation work. As a note, though some researchers have written of a "conservation social science," this term of course refers to the social sciences more generally, thereby obscuring the call for specifically sociological perspectives (Mascia et al. 2003; Bennett et al. 2017). However, these writings do internally pose many of the same arguments posed here for increased sociological intervention in species conservation research and practice.

A further semantic point must be made about the usefulness of aligning this work with "conservation biology," "conservation psychology," "conservation economics," and other actively (rather than passively) monikered research agendas rather than positioning this kind of work as a "sociology of species conservation." Sociology traditionally avoids intervention into the populations that it studies, and this tradition can and has carried over into existing sociological research around species conservation efforts. Simply, it is very much possible for sociologists to study social dynamics within a conservation effort without making any attempt to generate knowledge that will benefit the species at hand. That kind of work can be valuable, but it does not necessarily speak to the same scientific inquiry of a conservation sociology. Moreover, as it is normal and common that work in environmental sociology not be normatively environmentalist, the more passive label fails to call this into attention and to call explicitly for conservation science. Conservation sociology is a way of saying, "this is research that seeks to conserve species," just as conservation biology has been established as a conceptual indicator of the same.

How is Conservation Sociology Performed?

This section discusses the nuanced distinction between "conservation sociology" and the broader contribution of the social sciences, especially by parsing the differences between a sociological perspective and one that is rooted in anthropology, economics, psychology, history, political science, or other social science. In doing so, the discussion intends to in some detail articulate to broader audiences exactly what is meant by "sociological," as well as what exactly is imagined to be the essential sociological contributions made here. Environmental sociology can well contain conservation sociology within its disciplinary purview. However, it remains necessary to name and signal conservation sociology in order to render the social components of conservation efforts in a way that explicitly seeks to contribute knowledge for conservation action (as exemplified by the contributions of Chapters Three, Four, and Five). I imagine the contribution of conservation sociology as threefold: 1) to study the role of social forces, structures, norms and other distinctly sociological phenomena in species conservation; 2) to employ foundational sociological theory and contemporary environmental sociological theory, which is often specialized to the discipline; and 3) to employ sociological research methods, which vary significantly from the methods of other social sciences.

To the first point, it is the project of each chapter here not only to contribute research to the essential discussions of environmental sociology and to contribute a kind of applied knowledge to IMB conservation practice, but also to contribute to conservation biology a clear example of how a social constructivist epistemology can be incorporated into research of socioenvironmental phenomena. While the ontological claims[3] of such social constructivism are considered in some detail in Chapter Five, Chapters Three and Four make explicit epistemological examples of the usefulness of describing the social components of environmental issues such as conservation. This amounts to one humble example of the essential contribution of sociology: to acknowledge "the social" and to investigate "social things" such as social structure, institutions, and social forces. These social phenomena are frequently invisible, requiring statistical or in-depth cultural analysis to detect, much the same as cells require a microscope or some stars require a telescope to see. They are the focal point of sociology, and their acknowledgement represents a paradigmatic distinction. On the institutional level of analysis, for example, human individuals become component parts of the broader social structure, a shift in perspective that can grant organizations theoretical agency beyond what is assumed by psychology and anthropology. Sociology describes a tiered reality (micro-, meso-, and macro-) capable of accounting for the reciprocal processes by which individual social behaviors amount to affect social structure and how structures influence individual action. To the specific subject area of species conservation, sociology is yet to make its full offering. As detailed above, environmental sociological theories may have great usefulness in explaining social facets of conservation, but they remain largely untested in this particular context. Similarly, the more implicitly sociological research and findings of conservation biology have yet to take seriously the task of reconciling this work with foundational social theory, adopting a distinctly sociological perspective, or applying rigorous sociological methodology. Doing so would necessitate an explicit focus on structure, institutions, social forces, and the like.

Secondly, the sociological contribution to conservation may be further elaborated by extending the conversation beyond the abstraction of an epistemological and ontological disciplinary distinction to the more tangible distinction of theoretical foundations. Briefly, foundational sociological theory might be divided into three prominent schools of thought: functionalism, symbolic interactionism, and conflict theory. The competing theories of functionalism and conflict theory have (imperfect) analogues in environmental sociology in ecological modernization theory and ecological Marxism (including Treadmill of Production theory) (Mol et al. 2009; Foster et

---

[3] While some argue that social constructivism makes no ontological claim (Andrews 2012), this work adopts a critical realist position, which contextualizes constructivism within a broader ontological perspective (Danermark et al. 2005).

al. 2011). In the realm of conservation, we might distill this theoretical debate to a pair of dueling hypotheses: Does social development (e.g., industrialization) eventually reverse its now negative relationship with biodiversity? Or, does development perpetually accelerate an unsustainable relationship with the environment (e.g., unlimited resource extraction, unlimited byproducts of pollution)? In the field of conservation biology, this question remains far from answered. As demonstrated by environmental sociological research on carbon emissions and other socioenvironmental issues, there are a number of relevant complex structural, political, and cultural mechanisms to explore (Buttel 2003; Clark and York 2005; Foster et al. 2011). Conservation sociology can continue the task of contrasting the causes and consequences of extinction with other negative environmental outcomes, and of constructing models that position biodiversity loss and conservation within broader structural processes, as environmental sociologists have accomplished for issues such as carbon emissions, deforestation, etc.

Thirdly, the methodological distinction between sociology and the other social sciences is nuanced, but it merits acknowledgement, especially as it pertains to the social science surrounding conservation produced by those trained in the biophysical sciences rather than the social sciences. Again, in very brief terms, sociological research methods are typically sorted into qualitative and quantitative groupings. Quantitative work in sociology often relies on survey tools, and the rigor of sociological survey design is quite established. Furthermore, professional sociologists are almost always trained in advanced statistical methods for the analysis of data gleaned from these survey tools. Consequently, project by project, sociologists are able to discern with quite compelling empirical evidence incremental knowledge of social phenomena. This positivistic tradition is not mirrored in quite the same form in anthropology, political science, and other social sciences. The qualitative tradition, which (as described in Chapter One) favors a relativistic perspective, relying on ethnography, observation, interviews, etc., is tethered by intra-disciplinary cooperation to the positivistic tradition such that qualitative methods in sociology are less influenced by postmodernism compared to qualitative methods employed elsewhere in the social sciences. In lieu of an inclusivity of qualitative methodological explorations, sociology favors rich, detailed discussions of how to implement ethnographic and interview-based research tools with maximal validity and reliability. Thus, while no discipline's tactic is superior to another's, sociology's has evolved to be characterized by a quite intensely exact and scrupulous empiricism. Readers will note that while a great variety of issues are treated in this text, great care has been taken to not put forth suggestions that are unsubstantiated by data. For this reason, sociology is a natural bridge from the empiricism of the natural sciences toward an empirical conception of the social sciences.

With that said, there are some aspects of the research performed here that suggest conservation sociology may require methodological norms different in some ways from standard sociological norms. While social scientists frequently call for increased inclusion of knowledge(s) and a disruption of the traditional expert/lay stratification of knowledge particularly in the environmental context (Wynne 1996), the norm of understanding lay knowledge as interpretive or otherwise sub-factual persists widely (Petts and Brooks 2006). A sociologist that endeavors to take part in and study a conservation collaboration may study the perspectives of both the expert stakeholders and the lay public, but they may find themselves forced to present a stratified framework of knowledge in order to remain legitimate in the eyes of the expert participants. In these cases, all individuals' claims must be compared against the evident consensus—recorded or otherwise—and one who endeavors to present any alternative truth will likely find themselves discredited by other collaborators. The methodological solution is to adopt an inherently interdisciplinary approach by presenting conservation experts' knowledge as factual unless an equally scientific critique emerges (such a case is discussed in some detail in Chapter Three). Of course, this is no different than one's acceptance of findings emerging from elsewhere within one's own discipline, but it begs reflection in the present suggestion (emergent from the review of literature) for a more integrated, applied contribution on behalf of sociology to the study of conservation. I suggest that those creating this work might move toward integrating their contribution with interdisciplinary knowledge, much as ecologists and economists have established more substantial frameworks for sharing data (Ricklefs 2008). Additionally, the social sciences are well positioned to remind natural scientists of the wealth of research in support of increased representation of lay knowledge.

Another methodological distinction between conservation sociology and general sociological work is that environmental factors should be more readily considered data. This is one of the foundational distinctions of environmental sociology, and it is the reason I nest conservation sociology therein, rather than in sociology's considerable "animals and society" tradition of research. Just as scholars of environmental justice may use the toxicology of air or water as a dependent variable, scholars of conservation sociology must ground their environmental data somehow. In quantitative work, this grounding must take research beyond a near-exclusive use of the IUCN Red List as a biodiversity measure, toward use of on-the-ground data from conservation actors in consideration of specific species' cases. Biodiversity is a concept that is part of an exceedingly complex system of ecological research. By atomizing, or worse, using poorly linked stand-in variables, environmental sociological research on biodiversity loss and conservation may remain below normal standards of scientific research. In qualitative research, research might interpret not only the environmental within the social, but the social within the environmental. This means an expansion of what is considered data to include ecological products alongside human products—trade goods as well as their manifold environmental collateral; interviews and participant observation alongside the experiences of researchers in ethnographic observation of animals and other non-human life (Kirksey 2014); and visual evidence of environmental contours, especially through the use of photographic and video record-keeping.

Why Meaning, Power, and Time?

The substantive chapters presented in this book were each designed with three tasks in mind: 1) to tell a key part of the IMB's conservation story, 2) to present an essential topic that sociology can address in conservation, and 3) to demonstrate the various uses of conservation sociology. To the first point, while the Extended Case Method (ECM) is largely deductive, there remains a dialogue between data and theory, and emergent themes from the data are admitted into analysis. In this case, meaning, power, and time were the three most prominent themes found in the data. In other words, based on this study, they are three of the most significant social qualities of the IMB conservation effort.[4] To the second point, meaning, power, and time are all also essential topics of theory and research in sociology. As outlined in each chapter, the origins of these concepts are contemporaneous with the advent of sociological theory, each being excellent examples of the sort of "social facts" that Durkheim described in laying out the existence and nature of *sui generis* social phenomena. As such, it is the design of this text that each chapter make a basic, foundational contribution to the study of these essential concepts in the conservation realm—a starting place from which future research might grow. To the third point, each chapter also stands as an example of a different use of conservation sociology: description (Chapter Three regarding meaning), theory (Chapter Four regarding power), and application (Chapter Five regarding time). In order to make these examples explicit, each use is described in brief below. The resulting synthesis of these chapters is treated in Chapter Six, the Conclusion.

Chapter Three, which concerns meaning-making and knowledge, is a highly descriptive study. This piece organizes for readers the IMB conservation stakeholder network by actors' adherence to different yet equally coherent

---

[4] Other emergent themes that were clearly important but this study was not designed to address included gender, expert/lay knowledge, and public perception. Additional key social themes may exist in this context and require further research to identify and explicate.

sets of norms, values, and beliefs regarding the species and its conservation. Moreover, the chapter's conclusions are highly IMB-specific, generally concerning highly particular events and strategies in IMB conservation work. Though the piece engages with broader theory, it does so primarily to facilitate description. This is a demonstration of one of conservation sociology's possible contributions: the description of particular conservation contexts, compositions, actor networks, processes, problems, and other characteristics. This constitutes an important step in conservation sociology work, as one must at least partially inductively ascertain understanding of a particular conservation effort before one begins theorizing its components or prescribing applied solutions.

Chapter Four, which concerns social power, is a primarily theoretical study. In this chapter, theories of social power are used not only to describe the operation of power in IMB conservation, but to embed the IMB's case within a broader social context conceived by the aggregation of existing theory and research. In other words, this chapter situates IMB conservation within an overarching theoretical context, connecting thru-lines from a general political-economic system down to the level of the specific stakeholder group. Furthermore, the chapter seeks not only to use theory of social power, but to build upon it in the conservation context. Conclusions from this piece are more generalizable than those of Chapter Three, offering discussions of the form and process of contemporary conservation writ large, its role in contemporary civil society, and the inherent contradictions between the goals of conservation and limitless growth capitalism. These conclusions are also generally reflected in the total conclusions of the book. The chapter is meant to demonstrate another essential function of conservation sociology, which is to nest conservationism and conservation work within existing theory in (environmental) sociology, and to produce further theory as well.

Chapter Five, which concerns social and biophysical reckonings and accountings of time, is designed with an eye toward developing heuristics for applied sociology. Though time is both a highly specific topic and one that can be quite abstract, the chapter uses time as a concept to illustrate the unique ability of conservation sociology to identify, describe, and prescribe solutions to particular social obstacles in conservation work. Time (which emerged as a prominent theme) is used as a parameter with which to contain the analysis and discussion, yielding conclusions that are IMB-specific and solutions-oriented. Moreover, the chapter's design mirrors the basic use of conservation sociology to conservation actors: defining the social obstacles that exist in a particular conservation context and describing their solutions. In making this point, the chapter forgoes descriptive theory for a discussion of the ontological bases that render visible social phenomena to the conservation sociologist. In sum, this chapter demonstrates another fundamental use of conservation sociology, that of developing applied tactics for participating meaningfully in conservation collaborations.

Together, these three substantive chapters put forth not only a comprehensive account of the sociologically-relevant components of IMB conservation, but a multi-faceted demonstration of empirical, theoretical, and practical uses of conservation sociology. The chapters are concerned with disparate topics, some of which are at times highly interrelated (e.g. power and boundary work in meaning-making), while others are generally only linked by their concurrence in the IMB's case. Yet, this quality of sometimes-interrelatedness is resultant of the joint goals of telling the IMB's story and producing a coherent example of the uses of conservation sociology. Meaning, power, and time are only a few of the core sociological ideas that will be salient to the conservation context, and as further research is produced, these concepts will likely assume their positions among other essential social facts present in species conservation work.

Chapter 3

Describing Pluralized Conservationism(s): Positionality, Meaning-making, and Boundaries in Conservation Science and Action

It is a sunny early-autumn day in Lacey, WA, and I am sitting with a United States Fish and Wildlife Service (USFWS or FWS) employee in the grass of a clearing on the USFWS's Washington headquarters campus, surrounded by towering pines. The setting lends to a pensive conversation, and I ask if they will share some memories of their time working in Island Marble Butterfly (IMB) conservation. They fondly recollect friendly collaborations with colleagues at the National Parks Service (NPS), clever genomic research using butterfly feces, and breezy summer days at American Camp surrounded by IMBs in flight. Then, they pause. "The Latin name, *Euchloe ausonides insulanus*, means…" they say, slowly and carefully, "the good, green, gold - of spring - of the islands." For a moment, we are compelled to a silent reflection, practically enchanted by the evocation, the poetry of it swelling in me emotions I do not expect. I am confronted: What hidden, personal attachment does this reaction belie? What has the butterfly come to mean to me? I put it out of my mind to continue our talk, but I know that learning the secret of the IMB's name has only deepened a growing reverence, has only secured more of my loyalty. Objective and withdrawn as I may strive to remain in my researcher's role, I find that I, like the IMB stakeholders I have interviewed and spent time with, have assembled a system of values and beliefs that must necessarily be governing my total perception of the butterfly's circumstance.

This chapter explores the ways in which variable positionalities, experiences, and interpretive frameworks manifest shared and competing understandings of the butterfly, its conditions, and its conservation. To do so, the analysis employs boundary theory (Gieryn 1983, 1999; Star and Griesemer 1989) from the sociology of science and technology to interpret data gleaned from interviews, ethnography, and participant observation. The analysis reveals three broad ideal-types of IMB stakeholder, each associated with a set of values, beliefs, and norms that comprise disparate paradigms of cultural meanings associated with the IMB and its conservation. These paradigms compete for control of boundary object composition, boundary organization goals, and boundary work operations. As such, this chapter builds toward Chapter Four's explicit discussion of power in conservation work by elaborating the ways in which values and beliefs have circulated in and out of dominant positions in the conservation effort.

The chapter proceeds with a description of boundary theory, then an exploration of the three extant ideal-type paradigms described by the data, and finally a discussion of the implications of this descriptive analysis for IMB conservation and conservation sociology more generally. The chapter aims to answer two research questions in particular: How are conceptions of the IMB, its circumstances, and its conservation characterized among its stakeholders? How do disparate characterizations of these elements shape the collective conservation effort? For conservationists, self-reflection regarding values, beliefs, and norms may be a routine and necessary component of their work, but it is seldom possible for them to take real inventory of their collaborators' and colleagues' total perspectives. This chapter, as an example of conservation sociology in practice, demonstrates a descriptive empirical inventory of these significant yet understudied social factors. Furthermore, this inventory is meant for both applied and academic purposes, in both describing case-specific conditions related to IMB conservation and constructing a research design template for similar studies to be produced elsewhere in the broader conservation initiative. Lastly, in the context of this book, this chapter is positioned as such to continue detailing significant elements of the IMB's past and present conditions, to present prominently the perspectives of individuals involved in IMB conservation, and to consider and reconcile competing understandings of IMB issues, conflicts over which are some of most immediately and consistently remarkable social qualities of this case study. The "Boundary Infrastructure" section will be of particular interest to sociologists, while the remainder of the chapter may be of greater interest and accessibility to non-sociological audiences.

Boundary Infrastructure

Scholars of the sociology of science and technology frequently use a "boundary" model to understand the embeddedness of scientific production in the context of a broader social system (Harvey and Chrisman 1998; Guston 2001; Carr and Wilkinson 2005; Hoppe 2005; Kurath 2015). The premise of this model is essentially sociological and requires an understanding of scientific production and its social consequences not as pure outcomes of the logical foundations of scientific thought, but partially as products of social context.

Social boundaries exist between scientific institutions and non-scientific institutions (e.g., economic, political, civil, etc.) and also within scientific institutions (e.g., academic disciplines, private research and development programs, etc.). The present study concerns boundaries *within* a scientific collaboration. Scholars use conceptual terms to describe the components through which these boundaries manifest: actions and behaviors constitute "boundary work," products are "boundary objects," and liminal or bridging groups are "boundary organizations." Through these behaviors, the use of these objects, or the operations of these bridging organizations, social boundaries between groups are sustained and continually negotiated. These boundaries at once reaffirm distinctions between social groups and allow groups to effectively interface (Gieryn 1983, 1999).

Use of "boundaries" to understand the social world more broadly has become very popular in sociology,[1] but the model is particularly apt to describe the production of science because of the prominent role of science as a legitimate basis for admitting knowledge into collaborative decision-making processes in contemporary society (Jasanoff 1990). Developed across various topics and objects of inquiry by Gieryn (1983, 1999), Star and Griesemer (1989), and others (Moore 1996, Guston 2001), the boundary perspective on science need not necessarily comprise a theoretical extension of Latour's broader "Actor-Network Theory" of science and materiality in society (2005), though the frameworks can be nested well one into the other. To treat this issue in brief, theoretical conceptions of boundary things can (but need not) assert the agency of non-human things in social processes, and both theories rely on the same foundationally constructivist perspective on science. Scholars focused on the processes by which science becomes produced or influences policy benefit from a conceptualization of the active roles taken by objects, ideas, organizations, etc. at social boundaries in reciprocally shaping and being shaped by the actions of humans. However, scholars focused on outcomes and causal factors, particularly in applied contexts, may benefit from foregoing explicit use of an actor-network model, the agency of these objects, ideas, etc. being dynamic, irregular in scope, and difficult to operationalize. Focusing analysis on boundaries facilitates

---

[1] In particular, a more explicitly Bourdieusian and culturally oriented theory of boundaries in society has been popularized, particularly by Michele Lamont. The distinctions between Lamont's theory and that of Gieryn et al. are nuanced. Perhaps the best treatment of the issue comes from Lamont and Molnar (2002), who essentially nest Gieryn et al., despite any plain semantic similarities, as outstanding yet not entirely original influences amid a much broader conversation about social boundaries writ large across a variety of contexts. Here, Lamont's theory is not being used, and the text refers only to the scientific context.

understanding of the processes by which scientific knowledge is negotiated through a social context to produce social policy and social action. Boundary concepts can be dissected and elaborated upon in good detail. For the purpose here of positioning a theoretical framework capable of interpreting the ways in which disparate stakeholder groups negotiate meanings, myths, and facts, the broad essential concepts of boundary objects, work, and organizations suffice. It is important to define each of these concepts, consider their manifestation in the conservation context, and recall relevant findings from research using these concepts.

Firstly, *boundary work* refers to behaviors that sustain and negotiate distinctions between scientific groups and between scientific and non-scientific groups (Gieryn 1993). In the conservation context, boundary work may be exhibited by negotiations over conservation practices; use, critique, adaptation, or dissemination of boundary objects; sharing knowledge across social barriers; and defining science against non-science, among other actions. In the IMB's more particular context, boundary work takes forms such as producing IMB information for public consumption, inviting and prohibiting the public from participation in IMB conservation work or engagement in certain recreational activities, negotiations between conservation actors across institutional barriers or academic perspectives, the production and consumption of IMB research, and any other actions that result in the (re)definition of socially acknowledged demarcations between groups related to the conservation effort. Boundary work has been explicitly applied to conservation work, particularly to the co-production of knowledge in the conservation context (Rose 2014; Nel at al. 2015). Conservation scientists perhaps find the concept useful for its versatile and simple nature. It provides a basic framework that (not unexpectedly given its propositions) allows social scientists and natural scientists engaging in social scientific research to simplify the interactions of a great number of social institutions and perspectives by imagining these entities as having a kind of spatial existence, a model in which the borders of these spatial entities require a maintenance not wholly unlike the more familiar borders of yards, cities, and states. With regard to the boundary work of the sciences that attend to environmental phenomena, research has explored such varied topics as urban environmental policy (Owens et al. 2006), discourse in science-policy communication (Huitema and Turnhout 2009), and public health and environmental justice (Allen 2004).

Secondly, *boundary objects* are documents, materials, tools, products, goods, and anything else that might be found at the crux of two or more social groups, including abstract concepts (Star and Griesemer 1989). Indeed, this definition of boundary objects has become quite inclusive, a phenomenon that Susan L. Star, coiner of the term, explores in a 2011 essay with an expression of mixed feelings. Star argues that, yes, almost anything that exists can technically be analyzed for its purposes as a boundary object, but the concept is most useful at a particular scale: that of smaller social groups with set parameters, observable boundaries, and populations robust or consistent enough to foster internal discourse. Otherwise, the potential plurality of conceptions of a boundary object quickly trends toward a postmodern imagining of objects' infinitely divergent meanings among or even within particular individuals. In the specific realm of IMB conservation, examples of key boundary objects are peer-reviewed scientific articles; news articles and other public documents; material objects used in conservation such as fencing, containers, nets, etc.; spatial entities such as American Camp, perceived butterfly habitat, the prairie, etc.; and especially the butterfly subspecies itself. Investigations of boundary objects have explored such topics as the social construction of monarch butterflies (Gustafsson et al. 2015), re-conceptualizing "ecosystem services" at interdisciplinary boundaries to promote sustainability (Abson et al. 2014), the shared and disparate meanings of resilience as an interdisciplinary concept in sustainability research (Brand and Jax 2007), the co-production of science and practice in connectivity conservation (Wyborn 2015), the way artists and scientists divergently use the same materials (Halpern 2011), and more.

Thirdly, *boundary organizations* are those groups that operate in the liminal space between science and non-science, both bridging the gulf and maintaining the expert/lay divide that undergirds scientific legitimacy (Guston 2001). In the conservation realm, NGOs are exemplary boundary organizations, employing scientists yet engaging the lay public, relying on science for information yet working to disseminate that information in a way digestible to non-scientists, attempting to assert best practice conservation work that is informed by science, and sometimes very literally and self-consciously conceiving of their stated organizational purpose as being to do so (Franks 2010; Pham et al. 2010; Affolderbach et al. 2012; Gray 2016). In the IMB's context in particular, in addition to NGOs, one should also include the NPS at American Camp as a boundary organization, who despite being a federal agency that participates in scientific co-production in their own right, here also operates as more of a mediating force between other federal agencies, scientific entities such as universities, and the community of San Juan Island. Like the other two boundary concepts, boundary organizations have been explored in social studies of scientific, environmental knowledge in a wide variety of contexts (Guston 2001), from land-use management (Franks 2010; Cockburn et al. 2016), to water management (Kirchhoff et al. 2013), to climate change adaptation (Miller 2001; Brooke 2008) and beyond. There has also been substantial use of the boundary organization concept in conservation-specific research, including considerable investigation of local organizations' roles in turning conservation science to policy (Pham et al. 2010; Cook et al. 2013; Sarkki et al. 2013; Caine 2016), as well as the role of international NGOs in conservation work (Hastings 2011).

Though conservation work is primarily collaborative in its goals, the collaborative production of conservation works—whether scientific research, grant applications, implementation of conservation strategies, etc.—occur amid an explicit and implicit contestation of ideas. In this way, knowledge and meaning in science are coproduced among actors holding a variety of positions and perspectives. Use of boundary concepts gives language to describe the internal mechanisms of the process by which conservation science is thus socially constructed (e.g., the role and function of boundaries between organizations, the function of objects such as research articles, the influences that result in conservation practices, and the subsequent influence of action). Use of boundary concepts also tethers observations to more generalizable processes and outcomes found elsewhere in scientific production and in conservation science. In describing IMB conservation components with these concepts, phenomena within the IMB's case are made comparable and contrastable with other similar contexts. With these basic conceptions of these abstract boundary terms laid out, the chapter proceeds to a presentation of data before returning to their application in interpretation of the data in a discussion section.

Paradigms of Meaning Among IMB Stakeholders

Conservationists often share more than a common objective; they may share, for example, a respect for the advantages and contributions of science, a moral imperative to protect vulnerable non-human life, or a deep personal connection to the natural world. However, this does not mean that conservationists are a homogeneous lot. They come from a variety of backgrounds and experiences, express a great number of different socially relevant characteristics, arrive at conservation initiatives through a variety of channels, favor varied conservation practices, and come to articulate principles and aims in diverse fashions. This kind of plurality of positionalities has been researched a great deal by environmental sociologists as it pertains to demographic and cultural predictors of environmentalism more broadly, especially the effects of race, class, gender, vulnerability, age, location, and more on outcomes such as policy support, self-described environmentalism, opinions on climate change, and much more (Dunlap et al. 1993; Dunlap et al. 2001; Zahran et al. 2006; Dunlap and York 2008; McCright 2010). Although conservationism has not yet received the same level of academic treatment, it is logical to presume that conservationism is as diverse as broader environmentalism and that its diversity is meaningfully tied to the great many influencing social variables identified by environmental sociologists. Existing work describes the complex and varying impacts on conservationism by social variables such as gender (Agrawal and Gibson 2001; Tindall et al. 2003; Camou-Guerrero et al. 2008; Agarwal 2009), race and ethnicity (Agrawal and Gibson 2001; Schelhas 2002; Ojeda 2012), social class (Devall 1970; Mohai 1985; Haenn 2016), and more. To make sense of this complex plurality of perspectives as they pertain to IMB conservation, interview and ethnographic data were analyzed in multiple rounds of coding, aggregating patterns to an inventory of key expressions of value, belief, and norm. This patterning formed three ideal-type[2] "conservationisms," which are presented in detail in this section: "Skeptics," "Protectors," and "Collaborators."

These plural conservationisms are conceived of as resulting from a cocktail of lived social variables, informed by and subsequently informing values and norms in a dialectic of construction and use of the associated conservationism as a guiding paradigm. Importantly, this chapter argues that these influences appear to hold more sway than many of the binary factors cited by participants as being responsible for conflicts of ideas and interests in the conservation effort: government/non-government employment, expert/lay knowledge, experience/youth, biological/ecological educational background, tendency to egotism/modesty, etc. These factors did not reveal themselves through any pattern in the data used here as causal forces in the generation of disparate interpretations of the butterfly or its circumstance. However, I do not intend to deny their doubtless importance, only to say that as individual factors in an immensely complex concoction of relevant positional influences, their significance is at least diluted to the point of undetectability in this study. Further research, perhaps employing statistical methods, is required to understand these potential associations, which were indeed posited often by participants in explanation of individuals' differences of action and opinion. Lastly, though it is perhaps redundant given the empirical context of this research, it is important to reiterate that I do not mean to present any of the three perspectives detailed here as correct or as superior, such value-judgments being outside the purview of the science of sociology.

---

[2] For reference to non-sociologists, ideal-types are a kind of concept most associated with foundational sociological theorist Max Weber that are used to make sense of the social world by organizing its practically infinite variability into "pure" abstract categories (Rogers 1969). Though conceptually pure, these categories are not in actuality perfectly expressed in reality, nor are they perfectly mutually exclusive. Ideal-types are explicitly hypothetical, both hypothesized and hypothesizing.

The system of classification developed here is employed because it does help explain difference in opinion on some of what are identified as key issues. As the typology is described, readers who espouse a conservation ethic are invited to try an exercise of placing themselves into a single category. In this abstract exercise, one will likely find oneself in alignment with more than one category. Yet, it is at the sticking points of implementing real conservation strategies that will be discussed, such as a decision whether to capture and kill several butterflies for the purposes of scientific research, that one will find oneself forced to choose which belief most characterizes one's particular conservationism. Table 3.1 outlines these paradigms of IMB conservationism.

Table 3.1. Paradigms of Conservationism in IMB Conservation

	Protectors	**Skeptics**	**Collaborators**
Principal Value	Butterfly Well-being	Science	Cooperation
Core Belief	Best butterfly care precedes best conservation	Best science precedes best conservation	Best collaboration precedes best conservation
Conservation Norms	No research "Take," Mark-Release-Recapture, or other potential harm to individuals IMB taxonomy a secondary issue Butterfly conservation as prairie restoration and vice versa Small collaboration with trusted individuals desirable	Mark-Release-Recapture, Research "Take" Genomic taxonomy Opposition to secrecy Broad collaboration desirable	Seek peacemaker role Appeal to authority for knowledge; Trust in process Concern over ecological issues re: IMB conservation

The Skeptics

Interviews with what I here call Skeptics[3] shared remarkable similarities in mood, tempo, and substance. They tended to begin with an enthusiastic acceptance of the interview request, a friendly introduction on the date of the interview that would snowball so quickly into an IMB discussion that I would likely have to interrupt the participant to ask if I might turn on the recorder. Then would come, with very little prompting, an avalanche of strongly held opinions and candid anecdotes that would amount to an apparently previously conceived total narrative of just what exactly had "gone wrong" in IMB conservation, as well as the motivations of those responsible. Finally, I would emerge from a lengthy conversation with unearthed secrets, incompatible accounts of what should be scientific facts, and an empathy for the actions and beliefs of a conservation actor from whom some other had— in some cases deliberately albeit respectfully—taken care to direct me away. What, I would come to wonder, could have possibly caused the IMB conservation community to partially ostracize (or ostracize themselves from) a set of accomplished, passionate, and talented potential collaborators, clearly IMB advocates themselves? And, what did these outsiders, whose interviews felt so similar, hold in common?

In the recruitment process, Skeptics typically were recruited without a mediating contact, remaining either unmentioned by Collaborators and Protectors or mentioned briefly in order to indicate either that I should avoid incorporating their interview into the project or that they represented an antagonistic and even unenlightened perspective. Conversely, Skeptics spoke openly and often about Protectors in a frequently positive fashion, but one often hedged in an elaborate criticism. This criticism was consistent among Skeptics: Protectors may be well-meaning, hard-working, even brilliant, but share both an impractical risk aversion and a tendency to support conservation practices that will benefit their own career goals. For Skeptics, Protectors were sometimes used as a reference group with which to define themselves against. Overall, the group of Skeptics in IMB conservation were characterized by their holding science as a principal value and their core belief that science must precede quality conservation work. These qualities manifest through a set of associated conservation norms justified by placing

---

[3] While "skeptics" and "skepticism" is popularly used in environmental sociology to refer to the phenomenon of disbelief in climate change, the use here is rather meant to evoke the Hellenistic philosophical tradition of skepticism (it is also noteworthy that less ancient forms of philosophical skepticism may be more or less congruent with the "skepticism" IMB Skeptics put forth). In brief, this philosophical tradition is essentially a dedication to perpetual inquiry (Landesman and Meeks 2003).

science above other concerns: the use of mark-release-recapture (MRR) (also called "mark and recapture") methodology, opposition to secrecy, desire for genomic research on the IMB, concern for an inattention to the Sand-verbena moth,[4] and a desire to broaden the number of actors working on IMB conservation. I take each of these normative qualities in turn.

The use of mark-release-recapture (MRR) in a 2008 study funded by Fish and Wildlife Service (FWS) to research IMB population size, composition (e.g., sex), and movement behavior is one of the greatest controversies of the IMB's conservation history. While its opponents expressed alarm at its potential to harm individual butterflies and indeed the total IMB population, its proponents cited its regular and standard entomological application, its usefulness in comparison to sight-counting in developing empirical analyses of butterfly population and behavior, and its minimal risk. One stakeholder, Richard, who was involved in IMB conservation during the study and supported its application, explained MRR's value:

> You get a sense of dispersal [...] You know, okay well, they're at least moving this far between these populations. And you get a sense of how frequently different populations are exchanging individuals. You get a sense of whether these [...] locations are actually really more or less independent populations or whether they're functionally just one freely intermixing bunch. Which they didn't know at that point. And that's really important if you want to think about how to manage it, because if each one of these little locations is its own entity then the dynamics of the whole are gonna be a lot more decoupled than if they're all acting as one big population. So you could have a rise over there and a fall over there, and so that's gonna affect how you manage the populations as a group.

This quote summarizes the empirical contributions of the MRR method, but it is part of a larger conversation had with this stakeholder and several others about the costs and benefits of MRR, as well as the way these costs and benefits are differently perceived by stakeholders. Richard speculated about the opposition to MRR:

---

[4] The Sand-verbena moth (*Copablepharon fuscum*) is a severely threatened moth species whose habitat is limited to coastal prairie systems like those found at American Camp. Like the Island Marble, the Sand-verbena is thought to be on the edge of extinction, and American Camp is one of its only remaining known habitats.

I think personalities with regard to, uh, risk-aversion versus not risk-averse? And, how one values the potential information that one might get versus the risks that one might have from getting that information? So, you know the mark-release-recapture stuff is a good example. Yes, some butterflies could get hurt. [An FWS employee] hurt one. Um, so it can happen. And, yet, there was also a bunch of really valuable information in my view that came out of that work. And I think, um, some people would after the fact looking back on all that probably say even with that information, 'I still wouldn't want – that wouldn't have changed my mind had I known this was the information that could come out of it.'

In sum, Skeptics tended to bring up the MRR method in interviews as an example of the kind of entomological methodology that they perceived the broader IMB conservation collaboration as being averse to despite the detriment to total knowledge on IMB conservation resultant from its being left out. Ultimately, this single MRR study is the only one of its kind that has been performed on the IMB. Skeptics recall it as a moment of conflict, but one which resulted in some useful research with which to inform IMB conservation action.

Skeptics also expressed frustration with or overtly condemned secrecy in the IMB conservation collaboration. Skeptics were more likely to cite the historical existence of cliques in IMB work. Mostly, however, Skeptics expressed frustration with government secrecy in particular. One stakeholder, Arthur, described the consequences they perceived government secrecy as having in IMB conservation:

[An ecologist] found them out in the (*laughs*) on the part of the road where they set the fireworks off, with this tumble mustard growing on the edges of the road. (*sighs*) So he reported that to the state. The state reported it to US Fish and Wildlife which was the agency in charge of the Island Marble. Um, US Fish and Wildlife made a decision not to tell the landowner. The landowner's San Juan County. Partly Public Works, partly the Land Bank. They did not inform them. The County went ahead and approved the next year's fireworks. The firemen came out, dumped sand on the area that the butterflies were developing in, and apparently killed everything because the butterflies never came back. [...] And later, when we told the Land Bank and said, "Did you know that?" it was like, "What?! Why didn't they tell us?!" (*laughs*) You know, "We could have protected this! But nobody told us!" So. Anyway there was all this secrecy going on, one of which was that they wouldn't tell the school here that [an ecologist] had found a couple of little patches of eggs and larva on the school grounds. We found out and then challenged Fish and Wildlife to admit that to the school, which they wouldn't. And, then the school mowed the areas that had the butterflies in them. [...] A second population, a second occurrence destroyed by secrecy.

For Skeptics like Arthur, information-sharing, as one of the cornerstones of science, is extremely vital to conservation, and indeed its opposite, secrecy, can be and has been observably damaging to conservation efforts like the IMB's. Indeed, secrecy seemed more prevalent to the researcher than those who were not Skeptics seemed to allude. For example, in casual conversation, one stakeholder shared with me that they had heard rumor that the FWS was currently concealing information regarding the butterfly's subsistence beyond American Camp, though I did not seek to verify the claim out of respect for the conservation effort.

Another great controversy in IMB conservation's history is the issue of the butterfly's taxonomy. Skeptics argue that insufficient research has been conducted to qualify the butterfly for the subspecies placement it currently receives, citing the need for modern genomic taxonomic methodology instead of traditional taxonomy based on phenotypical observation. Further, Skeptics argue that they have objective reason for concern in the IMB's case, presenting evidence such as: the absence of known co-evolved parasitic predators such as wasps, which often exist for butterfly subspecies; the butterfly's mysterious absence for decades; Lepidoptera's famous ability to quickly change phenotypical qualities to match new surroundings and conditions; the IMB's close resemblance to the Large Marble Butterfly (*Euchloe ausonides*, the species of which the IMB is a subspecies) found prominently in the Cascades; a perceived unusual reluctance to conduct such genomic research; and the possibility that the butterfly may have arrived by hay barrel. For Skeptics, this was a critical issue, as the IMB approached its eventual federal listing under the ESA with the possibility unresolved that it is actually a population of Large Marble, a process by which large quantities of resources may be divested from other more deserving species in favor of IMB conservation. I became interested in the genomic question during the interview process and asked many of the final interviewees directly about the possibility.

To the latter concern expressed by Skeptics regarding the IMB's genomic question and subsequent conservation resource allocation, Skeptics—even those who were not particularly concerned with the butterfly's taxonomy—were more likely to express a specific concern about the Sand-verbena's position in the conservation queue. To these stakeholders, the lack of attention to the Sand-verbena was a troubling result of the IMB collaboration's powerful hold over American Camp's total conservation practices, a matter of species charisma and loyalty to a particular cause at the expense of others, and evidence of a kind of unscientific motivation in IMB work. One stakeholder, Ben, described trade-offs involved in IMB and Sand-verbena conservation to me:

> And so my fear is that the conservation effort to see if we can burn prairie and encourage habitat for the butterfly might actually be detrimental to the Sand-verbena moth, which in some ways is probably an entity that is more deserving of – you know, if we're interested in conserving evolutionary uniqueness, it's no doubt more unique from anything else than the Island Marble is, for me.

And so the issue for Skeptics is that especially without resolving the genomic question but also in general, favoring conservation activities such as prairie burns that may help the IMB at the cost of the Sand-verbena belie an unscientific approach to IMB conservation.

Lastly, Skeptics look to increase the number of actors and voices in IMB conservation. The issues of secrecy, of risk-aversion beyond the entomological norms, and of reluctance to acknowledge the Sand-verbena are for Skeptics tied to the small, tight-knit nature of IMB conservation. Many Skeptics, who have found themselves on the margins of IMB conservation, perceive the collaboration as a realm of power and conflict, of social forces operating at the expense of scientific progress as well as of research that could indeed benefit IMB conservation. For Skeptics, the more actors that are brought in from universities, from NGOs, and from outside the microcosm of San Juan Island and IMB conservation, the better science will be produced, the more accountable other stakeholders will become, and the better the chances the butterfly has to survive.

The Protectors

As described in Chapter One, the history of IMB conservation is characterized not only by two decades of far-reaching collaboration, but by the same duration of profound personal sacrifice on behalf of a few particular individuals.[5] Many (though not all) of these individuals are part of a group I

---

[5] For the sake of these individuals' privacy, I seek here to maintain ambiguity regarding the specific actions of those I may classify as Protectors. The IMB's conservation story and its total events are deserving of greater treatment than they receive here. This trade-off is necessary to make space for the present sociological discussion. A historical or journalistic account of the IMB's total conservation story, which can bring these individuals and their acts to light, is well-warranted.

call here Protectors, those stakeholders who professed a deep, complex emotional relationship with the IMB. Protectors share an expression of belief that in IMB conservation, ends cannot justify means. They stress that both individual butterfly life and the survival of the species are sacrosanct. Though most Protectors are themselves both scientists and key participants in the conservation collaboration, consideration of what is best for the butterfly supersedes both the production of scientific knowledge and cooperation with other IMB stakeholders.

In this research, Protectors played a gatekeeping role in attempting to allow or disallow my access to other IMB conservationists and the information they held. Interviews with Protectors were often difficult or impossible to schedule, and were characterized by a tense mood, an unwillingness to speak candidly on the record, and the participants' nervousness that this study might directly or indirectly negatively affect the butterfly conservation effort. A few Protectors declined interviews (either outright or through non-response), one citing fear and distrust. Protectors frequently suggested that I speak with a small, rarely changing, curated list of conservation actors, explaining that these select few knew what was *really* going on with IMB. They lauded other Protectors and occasionally denounced Skeptics and other outsiders. This group of IMB loyalists rely on a set of conservation norms that are consistent with their core belief that butterfly well-being must take precedent in order for best practice conservation to be realized. In particular, Protectors were commonly associated with norms of: insisting the unquestionable nature of the butterfly's uniqueness; decrying the use of "take," MRR, and other practices that may harm individual butterflies; describing IMB conservation and prairie restoration to be one and the same goal; and putting forth that IMB conservation is the result of immense effort and sacrifice on behalf of a few special individuals.

As described, Protectors often did not perceive any possibility that the IMB was not the distinct subspecies that had been lost to obscurity for ninety years before being rediscovered, as it is commonly purported to be. From my perspective, so great was the sense that certain individuals would react to my simply raising the IMB's genomic question by retreating from the interview or thereafter perceiving me as a sort of troublemaker that I sometimes shied away from approaching it. However, for even those Protectors who entertained the genomic question, these individuals expressed that the issue was ultimately unimportant. After all, the inability to list populations under the ESA only applies to insects,[6] and even if the IMB is genetically a "population," it would be one that expressed a unique phenotype, existed in a unique fashion among the islands, and occupied a unique ecological niche. Besides those Protectors who insisted on the issue or avoided it, there was one interview with a Protector, Juliet, who works for a government agency, who offered greater evidence in opposition to the Skeptics' position, directly attacking the hay bale hypothesis, and going even further:

> Mm, OK. So it's gonna come over on some dead grass. How many founders would we have? You have one butterfly that hatches out? Is it a male or is it a female? Is it born gravid? Does it eclose with fertile eggs? So if we have two - we have a male and a female. That's convenient. And they both eclose at the same time. I think males tend to eclose 4-7 days before females do. They only live somewhere between two and fourteen. The two chrysalises that manage to survive in a hay bale brought over from eastern Washington. […] Oh, those two - they happen to eclose in such a way that not only do they overlap, but they also mate. And then there's habitat available to the female. All of her offspring survive. I'm not saying it's not possible. I just find that very, very unlikely. Especially considering that people don't just bring hay to the island and let it sit around. […] Um, your question was, "have we found genetic evidence that the Island Marble Butterfly is its own subspecies." And my answer is that, first, the study was not designed to look at the taxonomy of the Island Marble Butterfly. That is not a question that the U.S. Fish & Wildlife Service investigates. We do not rewrite taxonomy. Um, if somebody else wants to rewrite it, we're fine with that. Now the data that have been produced by the study could easily be used to rewrite the taxonomy. And, if taxonomists used general rules of thumb, they would find that the mitochondrial molecule of the Island Marble Butterfly is different from the mitochondrial molecule of the Large Marble butterfly by about 2.5% if

---

[6] Indeed, this distinction dates to the Reagan presidency. Reagan, who described insects as "pests," tried to alter the ESA to preclude insects (Black 2012). Instead, a compromise was made that neither insect populations nor "pest insects" could be listed. For a tangible example of the subspecies/population distinction, the southern resident killer whales (SRKWs) that populate the water around the San Juan Islands are, genomically speaking, a population, yet their habit of remaining "residents" and consuming migratory salmon rather than migrating on hunting routes for seals as the more common "transient" orcas do, makes them ecologically unique and significant, and therefore warranting of their own ESA listing.

preliminary data analyses hold up. And that would mean that it could potentially be described as its own species.

Not only does Juliet refuse the Skeptics' their argument, she also cites research to the contrary, even suggesting the IMB could be a species rather than subspecies. This example is also useful in reiterating that I do not mean to suggest that Protectors are unscientific or irrational. On the contrary, these distinctions exist within and between scientific actors. Interestingly, however, it should be pointed out that no one else in the entire interview sample mentioned this recent genomic research, and many actors seemed entirely unaware of it, which does in a sense speak to the Skeptics' point of secrecy being a functional mechanism of Protectors' conservation action.

In addition, Protectors reject research methods that may cause the butterflies bodily harm, such as collecting live butterflies to be killed for anatomical research (also called "take") or MRR methods. Instead, Protectors advocate monitoring methods that rely on careful, extended observation, spot-count transect walking, and other non-invasive approaches. Another Protector, Leslie, thoroughly tackled the issues of MRR and "take" in butterfly research:

> That kind of work where you handle butterflies is not done on endangered butterflies. I mean you just don't *handle* it, because you have the possibility of basically killing an adult. There's a possibility, and it *did* happen with Island Marble. And if you have a population where its numbers are so low, you don't want to even chance some destruction of the reproductive form of the organism, right? So. It's just not done. But at that point in time - I guess how I want to put this in context - I think it was a situation where a couple people wanted some answers. And they wanted very specific answers. And they thought the only way they could get those answers were through numbers. Okay? Hence kind of science as this 'only valid information can be the number information,' okay? And that, um - they felt like they needed that, and that coupled with at that point in time, again, only very small numbers of adults in a couple places on San Juan and on Lopez. So there was this general feeling that Island Marble could handle it. I did not think that, and you can keep me on the record for that. I did not think that, and if somebody would have asked me then [or] asked me now, I think it was a mistake.

For Leslie, the use of MRR in IMB work was symptomatic of misunderstanding surrounding entomological norms, limited conceptions of scientific methods and data, recklessness, a lack of reflexivity among scientists, and other complex social factors. In this interview, Leslie's treatment of the MRR issue was elaborate, detailed, multi-faceted, and self-described as being a hugely important moment and aspect of their participation in IMB conservation for reasons that can here only be simplified for incorporation into total analysis. As the conversation continued, it moved from MRR to entomological "take" more broadly, Leslie describing how norms of her profession were at odds with conservation as well as empathy. In summarization, she told me plainly, "I could never *take* the Island Marble," spitting the word as if it gave her a foul taste to say it. As one further detail, readers will recall mention in the introduction of genomic testing on the butterfly using its feces. As traditional genomic methods would use the legs of butterflies and require taking several individuals, this compromise allowed the collaboration to finally conduct such research without harming individuals, as the Protectors had long successfully protested.

Protectors address the potential that IMB conservation could threaten greater ecological preservation in the San Juan Islands by reconciling the efforts: What is good for the IMB is good for the prairie, the opposite concern being a false dichotomy of choice. This holistic sort of perspective on conservation was a key part of the overall justification Protectors expressed for caring for individual butterflies, as well as other species. Protectors described a right to life, a connection between all living things, a kind of unifying force of nature and life that, if truly embraced, would be capable of relieving false obstacles to conservation that arise from an unwillingness to fully commit to the essence of the imperative. Science, were it to play to its fullest, would affirm that empathy and objectivity were not mutually exclusive. Matters of prairie ecology and butterfly biology were to be carefully monitored, but there was little sense in interviews with Protectors that real obstacles would arise, if other individuals, especially those Skeptics, would get on board with the Protectors' program. If not, they might at least cede decision-making power to those who care the most deeply.

Lastly, Protectors often and with gravity cite the immense sacrifice, effort, brilliance, and other extreme positive qualities of the few individuals they perceive as most responsible for the IMB's persistence. Protectors appear to bear, for themselves and one another, the responsibility for success in IMB conservation. They trust each other and are wary of outsiders. By putting the butterfly first, Protectors move toward a goal of enabling the IMB to achieve stability, livelihood, and ecological assimilation. For Protectors, my efforts were misguided in recruiting individuals from outside their in-group to my interview sample. After all, it was the Protectors who had saved the species and done so in spite of the interferences of the Skeptics, and outside perspectives would only serve to cloud the greater truth of IMB conservation.

The Collaborators

The largest contingent of IMB stakeholders is characterized less by a profound personal connection to the butterfly or a skeptical eye toward interferences in the production of science, but by a strong valuation of collaboration and compromise. These individuals, called here Collaborators, avoid taking sides with or against Protectors or Skeptics, value maintenance of a healthy state of partnership through peacemaking and compromise, and hold that such a collaboration yields the best possible quality knowledge and conservation action. As such, collaborators place enormous importance on boundary object documents, such as ESA listing decisions, peer-reviewed scientific articles, and news media reports that source prominent IMB stakeholders. When requesting a Collaborator's opinion on an IMB conservation issue, it is common that they will appeal to the authority of such documents in response (a phenomenon explored from another angle in Chapter Four). Yet, Collaborator's high regard for boundary objects does not extricate them from the boundary work through which they are developed. Indeed, Collaborators worked as authors on IMB ESA petitions, authored entomological IMB research, and more. Indeed, Collaborators were frequently both scientifically minded and personally invested in the IMB but varied from the other two categories primarily in their insistence that working together with others, taking part in a team, and resolving conflict were the necessary antecedents to successful conservation practice.

Collaborators had various approaches to dealing with conflict. Some Collaborators denied or were unaware that conflict was prevalent in IMB conservation, while others shrugged it off as an inevitable part of the process, even a functional one. Still, others fixated on conflict, arguing that their role as a peacemaker among ardent antagonism was crucial to the conservation effort. In general, then, Collaborators' perceptions of conflict and its importance varied greatly, yet they shared a commitment to neutrality in the face of conflict. This neutrality, while a vital motivator of collaborative exercise, is unsupported. That is, Collaborators regularly express values and beliefs that are inconsistent with those of the Protectors and/or Skeptics, suggesting that Collaborators maintain neutrality in part by avoiding confrontation on points of intellectual disagreement. Collaborators may disagree with Protectors, for example, on the importance of leaving decision-making up to the core group of experienced IMB stakeholders. I asked April, an entomologist who participated in authoring the IMB's ESA petition, about her lack of experience working with that particular species, and she explained her reasoning:

> Interviewer: Did you ever feel like, you know, you've never seen [an Island Marble], I'm not - not at all as a judgment on my part, but that it's weird to be writing [the petition]?

Participant: No. No, I didn't. I felt like I was writing it because I'm skilled at organizing data, communicating with scientists. At that point I was just doing a lot of that sort of reaching out to people who knew a lot more than I did about a given organism and who had all of these first-hand experiences with it and all the scientific data and then trying to compile that and get it out there in a format that was organized and accurate and hopefully could make a difference for the species. And a lot of times those scientists who are, you know, doing that data gathering don't have the time to pack it all up and give it to Fish and Wildlife Service or they might not even be able to do that for political reasons in their own job – or you know what I mean? So, no. That wasn't a problem for me. That was just part of my job.

For April, her participation in IMB conservation was by definition cooperative, relying on the accounts, data, and documents put forth by others. All of the underlying contestation that took place surrounding what kind of research should be conducted, who would conduct it, how it would be conducted, etc. did not factor into her experience, because she relied on the products that culminated for reference. These two qualities of imagining the purpose of her job as being cooperative participation and overcoming or circumventing moments of potential disagreement by appealing to collectively negotiated products were the hallmarks of Collaborators.

Another Collaborator who worked with NPS, Lauren, spoke of the role NPS currently had in IMB conservation:

I'm constantly amazed at people's level of commitment and the duration that some of these things and these conversations have taken place over time and it's – to me it seems like this is one of those things where it took a lot of dedication in pockets over many, many years to get to the point that we are, and so I think that the players that are currently grappling with, 'Where do we go now? What do we do? You know the butterfly's gonna get listed and we have to have a recovery plan and where's all the money and everything gonna come from?' There are a lot of people that have far more perspective than I do at this point.

After and before this moment in our conversation, Lauren would offer personal opinions on controversial issues in IMB conservation, from the Sand-verbena to history of conflict in IMB work, yet she would as well continue to offer statements like this one that ceded control of facts and narrative to others. It is not that Collaborators do not have their own opinions and perspectives on these key issues, but rather that they appear to value cooperation over those opinions. Instead of allowing themselves to be pushed to the margins of the collaboration because of strongly held beliefs or actively maintaining a desired in-group, collaborators seek to appease both sides by maintaining humility. Lauren also spoke of the NPS' need to work with others in conservation:

> When you can humble yourself and say, 'We don't know what we're doing. We need help, and we invite you in to be a partner with us in managing and stewarding resources'[...] There are communities and organizations who are desperate to provide their expertise and their energy to help these kinds of places.

In this moment, Lauren is speaking not only of Protectors but of Skeptics, those who are waiting still on the margins of IMB conservation, wanting to participate but excluded by their staunch positions. Collaborators then operate to appease Protectors and Skeptics alike by listening to them without taking sides, by constructing a neutral intermediary space that both Protectors and Skeptics can negotiate in without having to negotiate directly with one another.

For Collaborators, issues of prairie restoration, rabbit populations, IMB genetics, and any other concrete points of contestation boiled down to a process of give and take, a functional intermixing of ideas that would eventually work itself out. For Collaborators, inattention to the Sand-verbena moth is explained as a matter of belated intervention. I asked another Collaborator, Ethan, about the Sand-verbena:

> So having funding for both, you know, how do you make those decisions? Um, we still need to know more about the Sand-verbena moth. Um. I think more research is warranted. But there are certainly conservation actions we can be taking for that as well. We would love to be engaged in that *and* Island Marble, but again, it's the same players, so we kinda need to figure out whether there's a good functional group.

This quote demonstrates each of the hallmarks of Collaborator's conservationism: circumvention of conflict on a sensitive topic by insisting the issue will resolve, appealing to the authority of products of the collaboration, and lastly insistence that regardless of resources, science, and decisions, that a functioning cooperation between stakeholders was the path to resolution.

The IMB's genomic question is, for Collaborators, either a fair question that will eventually be answered, or, more commonly, it is a matter that was settled with the development of the original taxonomic definition. When I asked one Collaborator, Jim, about the genomic question, he offered a measured, wisely intoned response:

> Interviewer: Could I ask you quickly on that note, y'know I'm not a lepidopterist, but I'm wondering: are there sound methods for genetic testing to put that [genetic] question 'to bed' more or less? Could something-- is there something like that that exists or is it more about observing morphological differences?

> Participant: Good question. Um, the- I mean it's the right question obviously. We've been asking that for some time. The problem, Jon, is that DNA tests - depending on how much of the genome you get a look at - they tend to look at only a few genes. And if those genes don't show what you're looking for, then they don't. And if they only look at the mitochondrial DNA - the female-borne DNA - which is more often and more simply done, then that might or might not show the differences. So unless you get good luck with the genes you choose to look at or unless you are able to look at a wider array of the genome, that might or might not put anything to bed. And even when you get the genetic data, at the subspecies level, it doesn't necessarily put anything to bed. It's more helpful at the species level and certainly the genus level, but there's still - there's not a black box you put a bug into and it comes out and says what species or subspecies it is. There's still - just like morphology - there's still judgment calls involved.

A good deal of Collaborators echoed this kind of sentiment regarding the IMB's genomic question. Unlike Protectors, they saw the great usefulness of resolving the issue, but unlike Skeptics, they stopped short of becoming firmly invested in seeing it resolved. This quote is also useful in understanding the constructionism that goes into scientific taxonomic classification. While these classifications ultimately rely on individual or group decision-making made on best available knowledge, the result of such a classification becomes quickly reified culturally, and even legally as in the case of the ESA. What makes a butterfly a population or subspecies is for entomologists a negotiation within the scientific parameters of their discipline. Socially, however, that negotiation becomes interpreted as dogma. This phenomenon in itself evidences the social processes by and through which science is produced.

The prairie restoration/IMB restoration bifurcation is for Collaborators a give and take, a process of constant questioning and reflection, but also an issue that is certainly more troubling than it is for Protectors. They frequently cite concern for the ecological well-being of the total prairie, and rarely talk about individual butterflies, rabbits, or other species with real concern. Collaborators made jokes to laugh off the grim realities that manifest constantly in nature, and at times reminded themselves that the IMB's lot in life is in part pollinator, but also in part prey. One Collaborator, Carol, shared a related memory:

> Well I remember sitting down at Jakle's Lagoon down near Fourth of July Beach once, and there a number of Marbles out that day, flying around, and you know you really have to key in on it 'cause they look a lot like cabbage butterflies. But, there were certainly a lot of Marbles that day. And then, one of my favorite birds in the world, the Violet-Green Swallow, came along and nabbed one out of the air, and I thought, 'Ohhhh!!' (*laughs*) 'That's not good.' But of course that's part of life. And so that was – you know, that's one of those things where you stop and think, 'Uh huh. Everything's hinged on everything else.'

For these stakeholders, individual butterfly life and indeed the success of the IMB species must be nested in a broader understanding and appreciation of ecosystems and species' particular roles. And this, for them, is a very real concern, and though they negotiate frequently with the ideas of Protectors who seek to protect the maximum possible IMBs, they privately relinquish that high level of empathy in favor of a practical concern for ecosystem management.

In sum, Collaborators actively resolved the tensions embedded in the difficult sticking points with which IMB conservation is endowed through conservation practice. They conceived of their work as including, even in a prominent sense, the social work of negotiating and collaborating across differences with other stakeholders. The action of conservation work to Collaborators is in essence the work of maintaining healthy working relationships between individuals and organizations. Even when out in the field, counting butterflies or perhaps releasing them into the prairie, these stakeholders' labor was invested in reifying the consensus about best research and practices. They relied on others, made their ideas real and workable, but did not seek to supplant the consensus with any outside idea. Rather, they manifest consensus by conceding it to those who were able to manufacture it, motivated more to hold the working group together than to see it splinter into uncooperative factions.

Explaining Conflict in IMB Conservation

Having defined a typology of the paradigms governing IMB stakeholders' conservation values, norms, and beliefs, the chapter now turns to a discussion of the implication of this typology for interpreting boundary objects, work, and organizations, the potential evident explanatory variables governing individual attunement to a particular paradigm, and the contribution this research makes to current sociological debates. The use of boundary theory here gives name and purpose to the conflicts, debates, negotiations, and compromises central to the IMB's conservation collaboration. This theory, which is derived from the sociological study of science and technology, has been popularized in social studies of the environment and more specific issues such as conservation, because science is the common epistemological framework with which we interpret environmental problems. Understanding the process by which we come to know of and understand aspects of the natural environment requires understanding the process by which we create science. In contrast, broader theories such as Ulrich Beck's "risk society" are capable of contextualizing the perception of environmental problems (such as identification of an at-risk butterfly species) as part of a much larger societal trend of the instrumentalization of natural resources to the point of collectively experiencing "boomerang effects" that are then identified and addressed by political structures (Beck 1992). Instead, boundary theories of the production of science allow for in-depth analysis of the component negotiations by which a thing such as the IMB becomes an object of scientific inquiry, becomes labeled as a threatened species, and becomes symbolically significant to individuals and communities.

As IMB stakeholders commonly attested, it is science—not religion, superstition, history, or even politics—upon which conservation work is built. As well, it is *natural* science, as such projects as this play only a tangential role, no real norms yet existing for the inclusion of the social sciences in practical conservation work. As Scoville's recent sociological work on smelt conservation in California revealed (and this work partially supported), while conservation stakeholders are likely to express a desire for social scientific participation in their work, they rarely express strong social scientific literacy, and when pressed on the issue, often reveal a desire for economic models that confirm their presumptions about public behavior, rather than for sociological research (2017). It is worth reflecting from this meta-scientific perspective on the fact that this work and the interfacing moments of negotiation with IMB stakeholders therein is itself boundary work on my and their behalf. When, for example, a key IMB stakeholder declined my interview request by saying that they suspected I would write about interpersonal conflicts and that they could not see the use of it, they practiced the boundary work that keeps the social sciences from admittance to conservation efforts. Here, I am of course doing just as that stakeholder predicted, because I am confident that studying such conflict is precisely the kind of scientific inquiry that is valuable and needed at this crucial moment in conservation writ large. Concealing one's thoughts, attitudes, and beliefs behind a veil of objectivity is to the environmental sociologist one process by which we retain a false conception of the distinctions between the natural and social worlds. As I hope to reveal in this discussion, our social conflicts, compromises, and everything in between are vitally tied to the conservation behaviors and values that we espouse and enact.

This chapter has been organized to first present evidence that three ideal-type conservationisms are, in a rough realization of that abstraction, present in IMB work, and then to use this foundation to discuss the roles each of these conservationisms play in so-called boundary work. The chapter now turns to interpreting IMB conservation through the lens of boundary theory. In this space, boundaries exist between federal and state agencies, NGOs and government, experts and laypeople, the public and government, and more. Of specific interest here are those boundaries between the groups which espouse the paradigms outlined above—that is, the boundaries not between science and non-science, but within science. To reiterate, these groups and their boundaries were found to transcend organizational affiliation, educational background, age, gender, and other variables that one might expect to hold sway. Rather, I contend without asserting a causal direction that conservationists use and build these paradigms in a dialectical routine of informing their beliefs, values, norms, and actions. At the boundaries between these paradigms and their affiliates, conservation work becomes boundary work. For example, when a stakeholder implements a research strategy, it is negotiated by all actors, who weigh the strategy against their paradigm. At this moment, one conservationist considers the application of, for example, MRR and finds it well-warranted for its resultant scientific contribution. Another conservationist considers MRR and finds it deplorable for its potential harm to individual butterflies. And, yet another conservationist, seeing the conflict that brews, sets aside their personal opinion and engages in the social work of acting as a neutral intermediary, neither supporting nor seeking to prevent the strategy's implementation, finding the potential risk of interpersonal conflict greater than the risk of butterfly harm. Through informal conversations and formal meetings, both within and between parties, the process of boundary work yields an eventual result. Whether conflict or compromise, individuals engage with this moment not only using their paradigm as a reference but indeed further informing their associated conservationism. Like a process of political negotiation between Democrats and Republicans, regardless of outcome, members of both parties walk away more deeply entrenched in their position, spiraling deeper into bifurcation and polarity. The negotiation of a boundary point between groups is realized simultaneously with the reification of a group's values, norms, and beliefs.

The resultant scientific publications of the MRR study become boundary objects. Those proponents of MRR, when interviewed years later by a social scientist, speak of the material value of that study, while its opponents speak of the value of the research published using less invasive methodology. The work of science comes to have disparate meanings to scientists. Thus, as is the premise of this sociological investigation of science, one notes that science, being negotiated through a messy set of social structures and variables including beliefs and values, is not in its concrete actualization the realm of pure objectivity that it exists as in pure abstraction. Two scientists thus come to believe opposing sides of what should be fact, each arguing that they are using objectivity and empiricism to support their position. For example, the IMB's taxonomy becomes disputed. The theoretical usefulness of the boundary object concept is that it asks us to consider, "How is this material (or conceptual) thing disparately conceived and used?" When one applies that framework to IMB conservation and indeed to the *butterfly itself as a boundary object*, one immediately finds that the butterfly means vastly different things to different people, despite their shared singular goal of preventing its (sub)species from extinction. The synergy, then, of this typology of conservationisms and this boundary framework, is that it lays bare the pattern that explains different conceptualizations of the butterfly and its conservation, including associated beliefs, values, and norms, and indeed explains the presence and function of conflict in the collaboration. Conflict is profoundly linked to conservation work, and it is through studying—not turning away from—this fundamental process of conservation that we will learn how it functions and how to best utilize it toward achieving conservation outcomes. This is what conservation sociology is about. Instead of ignoring the thing right under our nose or positing homebrewed theories of risk-aversion, ecological vs. biological training, generationality, gender, etc., we must seek to *empirically* investigate this apparently grossly important phenomenon.

Importantly, however, though I speak of the function of conflict, I do not purport its position in a structural-functionalist[7] interpretation of IMB

---

[7] For non-sociological audiences, functionalism (or structural-functionalism) is a broad sociological perspective that imagines society as a system fundamentally organized to promote stability, each component part serving a purpose. An important characteristic of functionalism is that it is generally not critical of power and inequality, which the discussion here turns to consider. An alternative paradigm of sociological theory contends that conflict over scarce resources is a more effective organizing principle than stability.

conservation. On the contrary, conflict in IMB conservation is apparently a matter of internal power struggles that position one paradigm of conservationism in a leadership role, while disadvantaging the other to the margins. Protectors, for all intents and purposes, own IMB conservation. Collaborators operate most of the actual conservation work, but even in leadership positions, they do not advance an agenda antithetical to Protectors' outlook. Instead, they often look to Protectors for guidance. Skeptics, who once contested the center of IMB conservation and used that power to implement MRR, rabbit kills, and other strategies that Protectors disown, were at the time of this research at the margins of IMB conservation. Though Chapter Four will further investigate Power in IMB conservation, I wish to conclude this discussion of Meaning by linking it to Power.

Contemporary sociologist Isto Huvila writes of the investiture of social power into the production of boundary objects, arguing that investigations of boundary objects will reveal their eventual participation in the process of developing hegemony (2011). For Huvila, the interfacing and negotiating from which boundary objects develop are not consensual or neutral, but rather the operations of power. Boundary objects are in fact tools by which power is obtained, and the very existence of a consensus interpretation of a thing is a kind of victory of hegemonic thought. Boundary objects are by their definition tools of power, because at the moment they gain shared collective meaning, a perspective has won out. The IMB, as a boundary object, is such a tool of power within the conservation collaboration. One of the interview questions posed to most stakeholders was, "What does the Island Marble mean to you?" The result was not as varied as one might think. "Hope" was frequently the reply, or a variation on it, usually a kind of description of the unity of all living things, their right to life, and their special and unique characteristics. This is a victory of the Protectors. Several participants did reply that the IMB was a symbol to them of conflict, failure, and everything that can go wrong in conservation, and those Skeptical individuals were well on the margins of the conservation effort, despite whatever contribution they had once made. This is why genomic testing, butterfly take, and other practices are not currently described as needed or perceived as challenges. The butterfly has become sacrosanct. Its very meaning to its conservation stakeholders serves to invest Protectors with power over conservation decisions and actions. This transformation in the IMB's conservation may be symptomatic of a larger transformation in conservation science, by which conservation in the American context has come to follow a neoliberal logic, defaulting science and action as processes that prioritize conservation's social benefits and profitability (a matter explored further in Chapter Four) (Büscher et al. 2014). Science that calls into question a process of generating such benefits is undesirable under such a logic. Rather than a functional role,[8] conflict, I argue, plays in IMB conservation the role of negotiating boundaries toward the ends of developing a hegemonic realization of conservation action, materiality, and concepts, that renders greater control to those who seek it. Consequently, I recommend that scholars and stakeholders pay *very* close attention to conflict in conservation and indeed endeavor to as objectively as possible render its components completely clear, so that we avoid the intervention of political action in conservation work. Or, we may if possible openly utilize our conflicts to enhance our conservation efforts, by, as the Collaborators would have it, communicating as much and as frequently as possible, in recognition that power struggles and disagreements are not extra-scientific phenomena, but in fact necessary facts of science's production.

As a final note on positionality, I have said above that many of the suggested causal factors put forth by participants did not form patterns in the analysis (e.g., age did not seem to predict a stakeholder's conservationism paradigm). However, two such patterns did emerge enough to warrant discussion here: 1) NPS workers interviewed were more likely to be Collaborators, and 2) Protectors were more likely to be women than men.[9] To the first point, it is important to understand the history of the NPS's involvement in IMB conservation. While NPS is a vital ally to conservationist NGOs and governmental organizations nation-wide, its prominent participation in IMB conservation is unusual. American Camp is a historical park, and their infrastructure must be atypically adapted to this goal. They cannot devote all resources to IMB conservation, nor can they ignore the charge of the butterfly's presence on their land. They react by negotiating these pulls in separate directions by buying into IMB conservation without taking strong sides. Significantly, it is worth recalling that the uncooperative nature of particular past NPS employees has greatly influenced the values and actions of American Camp's staff (at the time of this research) toward a more deliberately cooperative role, according to their own testimonies (these actions are further discussed in Chapter Four). Moreover, conversations in related research suggest that the association may have some underlying, more generalizable roots, the NPS being a valued conservation collaborator in a variety of contexts (Budowski 1976; McNeely 1995; Burger 2000).

To the issue of gender, it is most useful to turn to the existing work from environmental sociology on the relationship between gender and environmentalism. Importantly, the current near-consensus on this issue is that particularly in the Western context women are frequently in art, media,

---

[8] "Functional" is here referring to the sociological theory of functionalism.
[9] To be clear, the analysis did not find that Skeptics were more likely to be men.

and discourse invested with a kind of magical quality of instinctual connection to Earth and nature. Indeed, women are more likely to espouse environmentalist positions and perform pro-environmental behavior (Hunter et al. 2004; Kennedy and Dzialo 2015). However, rather than a gender-essentialist understanding of this phenomenon, sociologists describe a process by which individuals become socialized to understand that a component part of performing womanhood can be outwardly expressing an environmentalist ethic. Moreover, this environmentalist ethic becomes linked to gendered divisions of labor (at work and home) and as well to broader paradigms of religion and ideology (ibid.). In conservation, we might expect the phenomenon to operate similarly. Protectors, then, are not more likely to be women than men because women instinctually care more for butterflies, but because the norms associated with masculinity and femininity in contemporary society influence individuals' expression of a conservation ethic. This discussion illustrates, in my opinion, not only the usefulness of this broader environmental sociological work in interpreting conservationism, but also the need for conservation-specific sociological research. We can partially apply our existing theory, but the particular context warrants its own conservation sociology.

Conclusion

These kinds of reflexive conversations about the coproduction of science highlight moments of contestation that reflect deeper disparities in beliefs, values, and norms. After the existence of these contests are empirically described, further empirical research can be developed to help settle disagreements and to further, more rapidly and more intelligently, the development of conservation science. For example, one stakeholder suggested that there was a paucity of research on the impact of butterfly "take" on butterfly populations. Lacunas in scientific research such as this occur non-randomly and are symptomatic of the social processes that result in scientific production. Issues must first be identified as warranting research for researchers to seek funding and devote resources toward their resolution. In this way, conservation sociology is well positioned to hold a mirror to other conservation scientists for the advancement of total research.

Furthermore, this work helps to embed conservation science in broader sociological theories of norms, positionality, and behavior in science. It raises questions about the application of social theory to the conservation context: How generalizable are these paradigms of conservationism? How are social factors such as gender, race, and class associated with the adoption of particular conservation norms? Does ideological conflict in conservation science serve more as a functional mechanism of scientific production or as a vehicle to develop inequalities of power and control? Further research is warranted and should be anticipated to have both academic and applied value. As a methodological point, while this research does not seek to quantify its essential concepts, they should be quite quantifiable, and future research should attempt to do so, particularly with survey tools.[10] A robust investigation of meaning-making and knowledge production in conservation work on behalf of sociologists may help to reconcile conservation actors with one another, as well as the objectivity of scientific production with the deep and vibrant empathy invested in the labor of protecting species from extinction.

---

[10] Resources permitting, I recommend applying survey tools with open-ended questions, then using content analysis methods to quantify responses. In this way, stakeholders may be given adequate time and space to formulate careful and detailed accounts of their thoughts and opinions. Transforming this information to quantifiable data increases opportunities for generalizing findings, particularly in the form of communicating data across disparate research projects. However, such content analysis methods should benefit from existing qualitative work.

Chapter 4

Theorizing Perceptions and Actualities of Power in Island Marble Butterfly Conservation

Aboard a mid-day ferry from Anacortes to Friday Harbor, WA, I am riding in the high deck cabin, eavesdropping on a few young men who are amongst themselves hashing out the contradictions inherent to veganism. Just then, a young woman approaches them. She sports a Sea Shepherd backpack in support of the international marine conservation non-profit organization based out of the San Juan Islands, famous for chasing and harassing Japanese whaling ships on the television show *Whale Wars*, among other radical actions in the name of animal rights. The young woman directly confronts them, voice shaking with passion as she recalls statistics in condemnation of the global-cycle environmental consequences of factory farming. Two of the young men become absorbed by their phones, leaving one to react alone. He immediately abandons his position, tries to agree with her, then changes the subject, asking, "You seem really knowledgeable. What should I take for a cold?" Seeing his diversion, the woman quickly, irritably apologizes and walks away. A stunned, tense silence persists for several long minutes, punctuated only by an embarrassed remark from the young man to his companions: "That'll teach me to run my big mouth" (Field Notes 9/17/18). We are headed to the San Juan Islands, where the non-human living world has garnered itself a small army of defenders and an authority that is not to be flippantly denied.

This moment of tension is both embedded and mirrored in the broader tensions of a political-economic context reckoning with urgent contemporary environmental consequences. There is no random coincidence to the Sea Shepherd's headquartering in Friday Harbor, the siting of this small conflict at the top of this Washington State Department of Transportation (WSDOT) ferry, the juxtaposition of two young people eager to hash out broad-scale enviro-political views, or my presence there in home of the Island Marble Butterfly (IMB), gathering social data to understand the function of power in species conservation. In that moment, our microcosm is nested with inextricable through-lines to the privilege and affluence of this wealthy, highly liberal northwest WA community, to a national context of Trump-era political bifurcation and polarity, and an international context of growing radical environmental ethic, action, and confrontation with established political-economic structures. Nested therein too is the IMB conservation effort and its successful Engendered Species Act (ESA) listing during the most environmentally negligent regime in recent American history.

This chapter explores the function of power in species conservation by analyzing the perceptions of power in conservation held by IMB stakeholders through the ecological-materialist lens of contemporary environmental sociology. The analysis relies on sociological explanations of power as a socially diffuse and multi-faceted phenomenon. Results describe a schism between perceptions of and actualities of two facets of power: decision-making power and ideological power. The chapter concludes with a discussion that explores evidence for causes of this schism found in environmental sociological research and interprets the implications of this schism for IMB conservation and species conservation work more broadly. The following section, which provides reviews of relevant theory and literature, will be of greater use to social scientists than other audiences, and though all may find the reviews helpful, the remainder of the chapter can be understood without formal sociological training.

Theorizing Power in Conservation Work

Popular sociological theories of power share a definitional quality: from an organizational perspective, power is decentralized among human individuals (Lukes 1986). This perspective is significantly distinct from what we might think of as the culturally dominant individualistic perspective that particularly characterizes the American context, in that the conception of power as person-to-person coercion (epitomized by violence) is specifically disqualified. Hannah Arendt treats this issue directly in her 1970 essay, *On Violence*:

> Power corresponds to the human ability not just to act but to act in concert. Power is never the property of an individual; it belongs to a group and remains in existence only so long as the group keeps together. When we say of somebody that he is "in power" we actually refer to his being empowered by a certain number of people to act in their name. The moment the group, from which the power originated to begin with (*potestas in populo*, without a people or group there is no power), disappears, 'his power' also vanishes. (p.27)

For Arendt, power through force is at odds with power through authority, which is garnered through consensus, as force divests the agency to concede power from those it seeks to enact power upon. Through authority, individuals are empowered by groups, while through force, groups are by definition relieved of the ability to endow individuals with authority. Though Arendt is offering a nuanced critique of Weber's foundational conception of 'authority', this essential conception of authority, force, and power is basically the sociological one. Sociologically speaking, power is fluid and diffuse, a kind of social force that operates through and between individuals, organizations, material products, and the natural environment. We detect power not at the moment in which one individual behaves in another's interest, but when interests become shared, legitimized, naturalized, reified, and willfully adopted. This essential distinction is echoed in the most prominent sociological descriptions of power: Gramsci's "hegemony" (Bates 1975), Foucault's "power-knowledge" (Foucault 1980), Weber's typology of "authority" (Spencer 1970), and more.

Besides offering an extensive theoretical accounting of the nature of social power, sociology also provides tools for breaking apart a monolithic conception of power to parse the distinct facets of the concept for more in-depth analysis. One such multi-faceted approach to power is presented by Steven Lukes, who develops an easily digested and disciplinarily versatile three-part categorization of dimensions of power: non-decision-making power, decision-making power, and ideological power (2005). Non-decision-making power is the force which legitimizes (or de-legitimizes) issues' existence in public or political discourse and that which grants some actors the capability to set agenda issues for debate, vote, or other decision-making process. Decision-making power is then the capacity granted to actors to cast votes or otherwise force a resolution on a particular issue. Lastly, ideological power describes the process by which certain ideas become socially shared and reified as desirable, natural, inevitable, or true. This third dimension provides an implicit critique of a binary non-decision/decision-making conception of power, as it allows for the interpretation of ideas *outside* of popular discourse to have the potential to circulate into the mainstream, or vice versa. This interpretive capacity applies to those imagined alternatives to extant social organizations (such as utopias), and therefore, as a conceptual tool, renders the radical what-could-be as real and as describable as the status quo that is (ibid.).

Theory of power in environmental sociology is woven into the fabric of the discipline, inseparable from inquiry in the field. The essential distinction between a "Human Exemptionalism Paradigm" (HEP) characterized by a conception of humanity as distinct and apart from the environment and a "New Ecological Paradigm" (NEP) that conceives of a humanity embedded in and a part of the environment implies a critique of ideological power. Like Lukes, Catton and Dunlap use the investigation of ideological power to call into question its permanency by substituting an alternative ideological paradigm (1978). The growth of environmental sociology and the rise of a substantial NEP in academia is testament to Lukes' argument that ideological power can be supplanted through the process of its critique. In this intellectual space, theory of power is manifold (Pellow and Brehm 2013). Where Catton and Dunlap began by applying their NEP to human social stratification, American environmental sociology has developed into a field characterized by a prominent environmental justice (EJ) perspective (1978). This EJ work was especially influenced by grassroots research, movements, and legal battles waged especially by the poor and people of color in the U.S., such as the work of the United Church of Christ in 1987. Sociologists of the environment study the politics of environmentalism (Meyer et al. 1997; Mitchell 2003; Johnson 2008; Breitmeier et al. 2011; Vasseur 2014; Sommerer and Lim 2016), develop cultural theories of the relation between class and environmental behavior (Stern et al. 1999; Stern 2000; Cordano et al. 2010; Kennedy et al. 2009; Laidley 2013), and use macro-sociological theories of "World Systems" or political economy to understand the function of power in global environmental phenomena such as climate change (Jorgenson 2006; Rice 2007; Clark and Foster 2009). Environmental sociology also has ties in places to ecofeminism and other feminist perspectives on the environment (Plumwood 1993; Gaard 2001; Mies and Shiva 2014; Kennedy and Dzialo 2015), which consider the intersection of gender, power, and nature. Lastly, environmental sociology also sometimes draws from the intellectual traditions of deep ecology, critical animal studies, and other perspectives explicitly critical of anthropocentrism (Smith 1999; Pellow and Brehm 2013; Pedersen and Stanescu 2014). We study power because the relationship between humanity and environment is richly laden with social power, both between human groups and between our species and others.

However, in the more interdisciplinary and natural-science oriented space of conservation biology, interpretations of social power can be rare, isolated, and incomplete. If one endeavors to conduct a literature review of theory of power in conservation biology, one finds quickly that the very word "power" is more likely to hold a mathematical definition in the discipline than a social one. Yet, what literature does exist in this space should be of as much interest to environmental sociologists as our work should be to conservation biologists. In a piece advocating investigation of political economy in conservation biology, Song and M'Gonigle (2001) cite part of an environmental sociologist's theory reading list: Beck, Latour, Giddens, Soya, Kuhn, Jasanoff. Yet, conspicuously absent in their discussion is mention of the theorists that come first to mind to an American environmental sociologist's organization of a political economy of the environment: Buttel, Foster, Schnaiberg, Gould, Pellow—even and especially Weber and Marx. The organization of this partial overlap of disciplines, which is evidenced in further research and writing in conservation biology (Czech 1998; Peterson et al. 2005; Brosius 2006; Peterson et al. 2006; Peterson et al. 2013), warrants its own meta-scientific study, though I will reiterate that a likely culprit is environmental sociology's inattention to conservation and biodiversity issues. Quite simply, with regard to theory of power, there is a great deal that sociology can yet offer conservation science. Lastly, the social sciences are not interchangeable, and the related work that is being done in conservation science favors economic and psychological perspectives on power over the sociological (an issue treated in detail in Chapter Two). This work attempts to begin the work of filling the lacuna of "conservation sociology" with a particularized application of sociological theory of power to the mutually interesting topic of IMB conservation.

The following analysis relies on Lukes' conceptualization of social power to organize a systematic comparison of the similarities and differences between perceptions of dimensions of power expressed by IMB stakeholders and the operations of power at those three dimensions conceived by environmental sociological research. The latter conception I will call "actuality," and I will support that claim with sociological theory and research throughout. Implied is a recognition that this "actuality" is biased toward the dominant perspectives offered by environmental sociology, which is of course the foundation of this text. Through this comparative analysis will emerge not only similar and competing perceptions/actualities of power, but a case study nested in a broader structural analysis. In other words, power in IMB conservation will be explored from the individual, to the collective, to the global, and back down again to the animal at hand.

Perceptions of Power in Island Marble Butterfly Conservation

Non-decision-making Power

When asked about the role of the public in IMB conservation, one stakeholder with decades of conservation experience working in state and federal environmental agencies, Steven, offered an explanation:

> I've been in meetings with legislators, and they say, 'Well, why are you doing this?' and I say 'Most people in Washington want us to conserve endangered species. That's what we're doing. We're a state agency. That's why we have these jobs. That's what we're here for. […] Most people in the state want that.' That's a very important thing to say. If most people in the state didn't want us to do that or only a minority of people wanted us to protect endangered species, this would be a very different conservation world. So I think the public role is to—when

those polls come out and they express support and interest, because that ultimately translates into the most important thing: our bottom line of our being involved.

For Steven, governmental conservation work relies on public support for continual legitimacy. This comment considers an idealized representative democracy that functions to translate public opinion into law and other mechanisms of effective self-governance. In this popular conception of the U.S. political system, tax dollars, for example, are funneled through state and federal environmental agencies toward accomplishing pro-environmental goals that reflect a pro-environmental will of the general public. Significantly, however, it is not to his peers or the public that he describes having to make this position clear, but to lawmakers. In this way, expert actors work to set a policy agenda they perceive as being legitimated by the lay public. I asked no IMB stakeholder where they believed legitimizing and agenda-setting power to lie, but through discussion of the roles of scientists, government, activists, and the public, a pattern emerged in stakeholders' perspectives on the issue: perceptually, the conservation agenda is set by conservation actors with the legitimating support of the public.

The synergistic relationship between public ethic and conservation action was similarly described by Anne, who operates a non-profit pro-environmental organization in the San Juan Islands:

You know, government doesn't like to take action against itself unless it absolutely must. And so that's where citizen actions are so important. Citizen activism is what defines our country in many ways. It did in 1776, and it still does in 2018. We've got to be willing to stand for things that are important to us. And here it's no different, and that's why I think the petition process is very critical to making sure public lands and private lands and critical habitat and species get an opportunity to thrive. Or at least live.

Anne echoes the perception of the public as holding a critical role in an ideal-type democracy, likening environmental activism to the colonial United States' secession from the British empire. American conservation is described as an act of manifest political will on behalf of the nation's public. In this perceptual model, conservationists are like public servants acting for the public good. And, it is through the petition process in particular that public will regarding a particular species' conservation becomes agenda.

An emphasis on ESA petitioning as an agenda-setting mechanism of use to conservation stakeholders was exhibited by conservation actors of all kinds.

William, who has great experience working closely with the ESA, described the key role of ESA petitioning:

> The way ESA is designed is that there's really two approaches that can be taken for a species to get into the listing process. As you've mentioned, one is the petition process. [...] Um, the second, and I would say at least—in my career least used—and I'll talk about why that probably is—is that the service itself—the agencies, both Fish and Wildlife Service and NOAA have the ability to just say, 'Hey we're going to go through a listing assessment for this species.' We don't have to be petitioned to do it. I think part of the reason that the agencies aren't using that latter approach more often is just because we have been so overcome by the number of petitions. [...] But I cannot recall any particular species on a 'species of concern' list that didn't get into the process through a petition.

As William points out, though it is not the only legal recourse, the citizen petition has become normalized as the only practical path by which a species becomes set as an agenda item for ESA listing consideration. Beyond the ESA, a stakeholder from the Xerces Society,[1] April, suggested that petitioning had set IMB not only as a governmental conservation agenda but as an entomological research agenda as well:

> From an insect point of view, Island Marble's been pretty well studied. And it was pretty well studied because of our petition, I will say. Not only because of our petition, but that got the ball rolling where people went, 'Ohh.' You know?

What kind of IMB research is performed and by whom is ultimately decided by a confluence of state and federal agents and academics through grant allocation, species access, and study design. ESA petition authors then use this research in further petition iterations to strengthen arguments for listing, in a reciprocal non-decision-making process of legitimization and agenda-setting. While one conservation activist with experience composing ESA listing petitions said of the 2002 IMB petition, "That petition if you look at it, it was pretty short and pretty straightforward, because there just wasn't a lot known," another stakeholder who also had experience in ESA petition work, Justin, summed up the 2014 petition quite oppositely:

---

[1] A North American non-profit environmental organization specializing in invertebrate conservation, and the source of the IMB's ESA petitions.

I mean I was writing petitions for species that had almost no available scientific literature, almost no data, like survey data documenting decline. A lot of times I was dealing with situations where the species was highly endemic, very rare, had very narrow life history or habitat requirements, and we knew that there was significant threat to that last remaining, you know—that stream where the only known population occurs [...] but not a lot of evidence that—or not a lot of survey work to document decline or even to make us completely sure that that was the only population. You know what I mean? Whereas the Island Marble, it's been so well surveyed. It's a large, fairly easy to identify butterfly, and in short, there's a ton of evidence to show that the species was at risk of extinction compared to some of the other species.

While early petitions may falter due to unavailable scientific research, they can motivate enough research to propel future petitions, when warranted. Indeed, IMB stakeholders cited the scientific, academic research on IMB taking place between 2004 and 2014 as a key reason for the success of the second petition.

Thus, IMB stakeholders describe a non-decision-making process by which expert actors translate perceived lay public support of a generalized conservation ethic into a localized IMB conservation agenda, enacted through research, policy, and implementation of conservation actions. This pattern was not disrupted in the data by any truly opposite perspective, though some stakeholders did offer substantially more nuanced discussions of ways in which the public may obstruct or facilitate conservation, the conditions predicting public support or opposition, and further such concerns. These issues are of great importance to governmental and NGO actors that work closely with the public, and readers of this kind may be disappointed to find the topic treated so cursorily here. Data for this analysis is limited in its representation of the public, as a design choice partially in recognition of the fact that the issue has been widely studied. Readers will find that existing research supports the notion that public/governmental and lay/expert relations are indeed nuanced as well as context- and content-dependent in their impacts on conservation (Cannon 1996; Press et al. 1996; Czech and Krausman 2001; Manfredo et al. 2003; Teel and Manfredo 2010).

Decision-making Power

Conservation collaborations like the IMB's are rife with significant moments of formal decision-making. The all-important ESA listing decision is exemplary (the ESA having a 99% success rate so far of preventing the extinction of listed species, though factors such as bias in species coverage do complicate this statistic) (Schwartz 2008; Center for Biological Diversity 2019), but there are also research design choices, implementations of conservation strategies, allocations of funds, and decisions whether to disclose or withhold information. Perceptions of particular decisions varied widely (as explored in Chapter Three), especially by individuals' professional and personal proximity to the decision-maker(s). For example, those who joined the IMB conservation effort years after a key decision were likely to express confusion or apathy toward that decision, while those who had supported or opposed the decision in their own memory were likely to hold strong opinions. However, of the formal, general decision-making process, participants expressed a consistent pattern of perception: When expressing agreement with a conservation decision, IMB stakeholders tend to talk about decision-making power as a cooperative, institutionalized process. When the decision in question was a point of frustration, it tended to be attributed to a single (or few) individual's rogue interference.

Examples of this perception were common in the interview process, but this point being part of a larger discussion, I will limit interview data presentation to three clear examples. First, when asked about how the Fish and Wildlife Service (FWS) makes final listing decisions, a stakeholder with FWS, Ben, explained the nuanced legality by which a decision is justified:

> The way the act is designed, you can only make a decision about the listing of a species solely based on [science]. I should actually read it from the act. [...] Okay, so in terms of listing determinations, it says 'the secretary'—although the listing decision, that usually gets deferred to the director—'shall make determinations [...] solely on the basis of the best scientific and commercial data available.' [...] So for a listing decision, they essentially have to look at the science. Now obviously there's some interpretation on that. But they can't look at economic factors. They can't look at social factors. They can't look at, you know, is this going to affect more private land than federal land. That cannot come into play in terms of a listing determination of whether the species warrants protection under the act.

Ben went on to further explain the important semantic distinction implied by the term "available science," which implies science that has been peer-reviewed and published and not hypothetical studies that might take place at some time.[2] These distinctions are informative, but they also imply the kind of collective, organizational perspective many stakeholders hold toward decision-making processes in conservation work. By the word of the law and the standards of science and conservation, no individual shall put speculation about social impacts, potential conflicts, etc. above the natural science that indicates a particular species' threat of extinction.

Secondly, outside of the ESA listing process, the implementation of general conservation action is similarly regarded as the result of collective decision-making. In conversation with one stakeholder, Deborah, they simultaneously described conservation action as collectively wrought while decrying the actions of individuals for moments of conservation inaction. Citing another conservation scholar's poignant turn of phrase, Deborah told me:

> She said that the hardest pivot of her understanding of conservation biology was that it wasn't conservation biology. It's *conversation* biology. I always liked that line. It's conversation biology. I find that when you are working with other conservation biologists, that when you do not identify a clear goal and then discuss how each person supports reaching that goal, that conservation becomes nearly impossible. One of the biggest complicating factors that I run into with every single species I have worked on is that there are people who, for whatever reason, want to be the center of the effort and be seen as—and I'm projecting this—I think that they want to be seen as the saving grace of a species. And in many instances, it leads to people controlling access to information, um, not providing all of the information, uh, slowing down timelines, uh, disparaging the opinions of others, and not being able to admit when they are wrong. And I connect all of those things to ego. And I feel that intellectual humility is the key to all scientific progress, especially when it comes to conservation. And in the absence of that humility, we cultivate interpersonal dynamics that don't allow for a collaborative process to develop. And that hinders conservation.

Deborah succinctly summarizes what is the commonly held perception among IMB stakeholders of decision-making: it must be collective to have positive results, and individually wrought decisions are disruptive, even inherently anti-conservationist. It is important to note now that this research

---

[2] One reason why this distinction is salient is that by this reading, a species must be proven to be already threatened to merit listing, thus contributing to listing delay in the cases of species that may be understudied or may not yet be threatened despite being in a state of rapid decline.

does not find this position to be arbitrary or incoherent. On the contrary and as will be explored further in the next section of this chapter, it makes quite a bit of sense, being that our established social channels for conservation decision-making depend upon legal and other institutional norms that enforce a collective decision-making process. However, what this analysis will challenge is the implication of "ego," a psychological perspective and one which can be supplanted with a sociological perspective that implicates distinctions in social power. In particular, the analysis suggests that individual decisions with disruptive consequences are in fact a feature of the organizational structures that currently govern species protection.

As one final example, it is worth looking at a moment in which an interview participant explicitly blamed specific individuals for patterns of failure in IMB conservation. The example should be prefaced with the fact that finger-pointing was relatively inconsistent in the sample, and that there was no individual implicated by one participant who was not also vehemently defended by another participant. In this example, one stakeholder, Matthew, rails against perceived careerism and its impact on IMB conservation:

> So somebody's made an entire career off of this, without actually saving the organism and indeed having made decisions like continuing a study while the deer were eating the —that led to their extirpation from one of the two properties where there was a substantial population to begin with. And, that's not a very good signal to young scientists, that the way to have a really good career is to find some threatened organism somewhere, study it literally to death, and then be the only person who—it's what anthropologists used to do with primitive tribes is study them to death, and then be the only person who could lecture about them because no one had ever been able to talk to them! (*Laughs*) It's just the same kind of baloney where that's absolute career security, is to study something that no longer exists. You're the only one who got to see it. So, um, it's just a terrible story of conservation being about people and people's careers and people's personal needs and people's personal conflicts and such.

While that psychological term "ego" was very commonly and organically brought up by participants, what is unique and fascinating about this individual's perspective on others' failures in decision-making is that they blame individuals without blaming individuals. Careerism is for this stakeholder a kind of force into which the individuals in question are swept up, caught in a process that rewards autonomy, ownership over one's object of research, and exclusion of others from the research and conservation processes. It is not quite a counterpoint to the individualization of harmful decision-making, but a kind of organizational perspective on that phenomenon. The pattern of blaming individuals for failures of decision-making in IMB conservation is remarkably consistent enough to permeate the perspectives of even participants who are explicitly institutionally minded.

Analysis found two important exceptions to this larger pattern. First, when refusing to provide a personal opinion on a particular decision, individuals often referred to formal documents such as the ESA listing decision. In these cases, the interview participant effectively abstracts the decision-making process from decision-makers, assigning an *ex nihilo* authority to the decision itself. This was done especially when individuals sought to speak on behalf of their organization or of the full collective of IMB stakeholders. In this way, the decision is not specifically attributed to a collective decision-making process. Rather, the collectivity of the process is implied by the erasure of individuals' agency. In one interview, a governmental conservation actor held fast to the company line when pressed for a perspective on the 2004 negative listing decision, refusing repeatedly to offer any personal recollection of the matter and insisting that I review official records. Even when I told them I had reviewed said records and explicitly sought their personal opinion, they defended their position on the subject by insisting it would be best to retrieve the documents and review them together. This stakeholder, who was active in IMB conservation at the time of the decision, implied in this encounter that the decision's documented form is, teleologically, one and the same with its process of becoming. And, for practical purposes, this may be both often true and an understandable professional response to inquiry. However, in attempting to better understand the decision-making process, one might interpret this type of response as an omission of perspective, if not a subtle form of evidence that the decision-making process is perceived as collectively accomplished.

The second exception was that individuals reflecting with approval upon their own decisions tended to refer to those decisions as informed by compromise and collaboration but ultimately a result of their own judgment. Never in any interview did an individual express regret or remorse for a specific past decision related to IMB conservation, though I generally made a rule of not corrupting the interview data by prodding sensitive decisions outright with their decision-makers, and individuals did express regret over past disagreements and other factors not directly related to decision-making. Instead, decision-makers who recounted their past choices tended to do so with optimism. In this example, Nora, who stepped into a leadership role, reflects on her ability to help navigate the personalities and egos they held responsible for dysfunction in IMB conservation:

[There were] a couple of strong personality people on either side. And they just rubbed each other the wrong way. So when I got there—when I arrived at San Juan Island—that was kind of the state of affairs. There were misunderstandings and, well, kind of a lack of trust and resentment on both sides and things were kinda paralyzed actually. But I think on the time that I was there we were able to really resolve that. So when I look back on my time as the [*redacted*], one of the things I'm actually most proud of is the way we righted that ship and got everybody on the same page and back together again, really doing significant work to conserve the butterfly.

While Nora does blame other specific individuals for conservation malfeasance, she gives herself partial credit for relieving the conflict. Interestingly, Nora does transition away from using "I" to using "we" at the end of this quote, at which point she begins participating in that consistent pattern of describing successes as ultimately a matter of collective action. Conservation, as it were, is a space in which individuals can achieve personal success and feel personal pride, yet its impacts are ultimately remembered to be well beyond the individual.

So, description of the decision-making process varied by individuals' proximity to the decisions in question, their choices whether to speak as individuals or on behalf of their parent organization, and whether or not they viewed the decision favorably. In a rough pattern, stakeholders observably portrayed the decision-making process as collective when in agreement with the outcome and as individual when in disagreement. In general, if stakeholders weighed in on past decisions, they tended to dole blame to others and/or tout their own accomplishments. Summarily, the power to choose—to set and enforce policy, to set a research project in motion, to implement a conservation strategy, etc.—is flexibly located by IMB stakeholders between the individual and the collective, apparently determined by criteria of positionality. This decision-making flexibility and its mechanics are considered in the section below on Actualities of Power.

Ideological Power

It is tricky to assemble a clear picture of what "perceptions of ideological power in IMB conservation" look like. Challenges are presented by the abstract nature of ideology, its plurality of form, and the subliminal nature of its influence on individuals' expression of thought and opinion. To organize the discussions of perception and actuality of ideological power, I ground the discussion in Gramsci's concept of hegemony. In brief, Gramsci distinguished between the political-economic structure of capitalism and the sphere of civil society, in which NGOs, the media, universities, and other actors developed the knowledge and culture through which the bourgeoisie manufacture legitimating consent for the governance of the capitalist structure (Buttigieg 1995; Gramsci 1992-2007). This phenomenon of culture and knowledge in pursuit of capitalist structural maintenance is called "hegemony." To be clear on the relationship between the two concepts, hegemony is essentially the dominant ideology of capitalism operating in the civil sphere (ibid.).

In the contemporary American context, conservation is expressly the enterprise of civil society, the preservation of biodiversity being an industry mostly populated by NGOs, universities, volunteers, and local government. In the section below on Actualities of Power, the role conservation plays in Gramsci's model of social power is further explored, but the chapter now proceeds by setting hegemony as the standard by which to detect perceptions of ideological power. To reiterate, hegemony will manifest as ideas, beliefs, values, norms, and other aspects of culture and knowledge produced by civil society that reify bourgeois supremacy as well as the naturalness, inevitability, and goodness of the industrial capitalist structure. By this definition, I accept three kinds of interview-based evidence. First, if a participant mentions ideology outright and of their own accord, this is a direct accounting of the issue. Second, I consider descriptions of the contemporary political-economic system as natural, as inevitable, as inherently good, or as unlikely to change to be evidence of perceiving such an ideological power. Third, evidence of ideological power can be found in support for contemporary industrial capitalism and its ability to solve or contribute positively to conservation. I mentioned neither capitalism nor ideology to any interview participant. Yet, their perceptions of this issue are revealed in their articulations of the components of ideology, and in their silence on the core issue itself. I turn first to naturalness, inevitability, and support for market solutions, then to the issue of silence toward ideology, and then lastly to explicit mention.

The inevitability and naturalness of our capitalist economic system was most commonly demonstrated in discussions of housing, tourism, and land-use trends in the San Juan community. These issues were talked about as fundamentally salient to IMB conservation, but unlike local ecological concerns, biological concerns, or even global-scale concerns such as climate change, IMB stakeholders rarely expressed the sense that these economic forces were preventable or negotiable in any way. Instead, they appeared to see them as existential transformations that efforts to conserve butterflies, restore prairies, or conserve biodiversity broadly must simply endure. IMB stakeholders were not unconcerned about these economic transformations, but they were roundly uncritical of their relationship to conservation work.

One stakeholder, Diane, described the problem of limited affordable housing on San Juan Island:

> I think that the tourism economy has brought a lot of people here becoming interested in second home ownership and retirement. So, there's a constant influx of new transplants into the island, many of whom are pretty well off. And then there's the whole service sector of— there's people who are struggling out here. Affordable housing is a problem everywhere, and it's no different here in that the tourism-based economy has really tapped the private housing market, turned a lot of those what would have otherwise been long-term rentals into vacation rentals and so working people can't even find places to live, literally.

Indeed, when one spends time driving the roadways, side-streets, and back-roads of San Juan Island, one does get the sense that affordable housing may be limited. Moreover, Diane notes that the phenomenon is associated with several impacts, concerns that were echoed by many other stakeholders: rapid residential turnover, a need for service workers without an infrastructure for them, a transformation of the basis of the San Juan Islands' economy, and the transformation of multi-functional land-space into expensive private housing or rental housing. And, what is quite remarkable is that this was presented time and again by stakeholders as a sort of abstraction—a "wave," a "turning point," a "sea change"—yet it is no exaggeration to call human transformation of the natural landscape the most powerful and transformative thing occurring at or around the IMB's conservation effort. One stakeholder even suggested that the very existence of American Camp may well be owed less to the community's appreciation of its historical significance than that fact being a useful excuse by which the community was able to insulate a small portion of their island from mansion and estate construction. Indeed, the IMB very clearly clings to the tip of an island that has been transformed by capitalist forces— agricultural, residential, or eco-tourist—away from coastal prairie habitat and toward an economically oriented landscape uninhabitable to the insect.

From a positivist position, the silence of an interview sample on a particular issue is strictly an absence of data, and so readers are reminded of the interpretivist methodological framework established by Burawoy that undergirds the extended case methodology (ECM) applied here (Burawoy 1998). Indeed, further research is required to comment on IMB stakeholders' attitudes toward political economy or capitalism more specifically. Still, in having held in-depth interviews with stakeholders in which quite broad questions were posed regarding the existential threats related to society faced by IMBs, it became a pattern of its own that stakeholders should remain almost entirely silent regarding a political economy that is being contemporaneously, explicitly implicated in biodiversity issues by social movements, politicians, and scholars. Attending to silences and absences is an old and established trick of feminist and other critical perspectives, who argue that as much may be gleaned from their investigation (Becker 2000). In this case, patterned omission of political economy from what were varied and general discussions of socioenvironmental relations in IMB conservation evidences the certainty, normalcy, and ubiquity of capitalism achieved by hegemony's operation in the civil sector. In extensive, varied conversations with IMB stakeholders regarding social contributors to biodiversity loss and social constraints to conservation practice, capitalism, as we should expect, was perhaps not exactly invisible, but was certainly hidden.

An important caveat to this point is the singular interview in which a participant cited capitalism and of their own accord described a political-economic force operating in opposition to conservation. This participant, Margaret, who is a private resident of the San Juan Islands, responded to a question about the absence of First Nations representation from IMB negotiations by describing a big-picture frustration:

> I mean, you know if you look at the big picture [...] we're bringing the planet to its death for God's sake. I feel like my generation should be thoroughly ashamed of itself, but then once again, there's been so much deception and duplicity. You know my book [...] is all about the corporatization of consciousness and the way capitalism destroyed communism and is also destroying democracy. So, it's all become a follow-the-money journey. And, the disaster's just global in horrific ways.

Having authored a book on a related issue, Margaret was uniquely positioned by their background to put forth a perspective that was otherwise left unsaid in the interview sample. Indeed, it is unlikely based on the commonality of political jokes, hippie-like self-identification, and strongly held environmentalist values expressed by some stakeholders that this individual represents the singular anti-capitalist sentiment held among IMB conservationists. Rather, one must look to the inherently covert nature of hegemony for an explanation of its absence from formal conservation discussion, a phenomenon discussed in the section below further regarding ideology.

Actualities of Power in IMB Conservation

Demonstration of disparity between common perception and actuality is a proven utility of the sociological (and indeed scientific) perspective. Immersed in our social worlds, perceptually limited, and confined to our immediate presents, we are often unable to detect patterns and trends that are rendered visible by statistical and other empirical analyses. For example, the social category of "race," while very real in its observable social consequences, collapses under scientific scrutiny. Sociologically, the malleability of racial categories as well as their fluidity by time and place evidence their socially constructed nature. Moreover, and in an interdisciplinary vein, biological research reveals that within-race genetic variability is at least indistinct from between-race genetic variability (Livingstone and Dobzhansky 1962). In this example, our collective acknowledgement of the fact's precedence over the myth can have profound social consequences, especially by undermining the credibility and internal logic of racism. In studying power in IMB conservation, the stakes are quite a bit more limited in scope, yet similarly approaching the rift between perception and actuality, especially from an interdisciplinary perspective, can help to supplant myth with fact. In particular, I find that while IMB stakeholders' perceptions of non-decision-making power are empirically substantiated, their perceptions of decision-making power and ideological power vary meaningfully from the actuality supported by contemporary theory and research and, in some cases, the shared historical accounts of stakeholders. Of decision-making power, this exercise reveals the role of collective authority in obscuring moments in which individuals exert force. Of ideological power, the exercise implicates the hegemonic functions of conservation, which absolve capitalism, compartmentalize pro-ecological behavior, and instrumentalize conservation for the maintenance of bourgeois boundaries.

While interview data paints a picture of perceived power in IMB conservation, describing the actualities of power must rely on relevant empirical observation, peer-reviewed research, and events records. It is unfortunate but not unexpected that the research presented here is as of yet the only sociological research conducted on IMB conservation specifically. Yet, a substantial body of research from environmental sociology, conservation biology, and beyond amounts to a coherent description of the actualities of power and politics in species conservation writ large. This reliance on broader research also brings an opportunity to understand and theoretically embed the IMB's case in the wider context. This discussion again follows the simple theoretical organization of considering each of Lukes' dimensions of power in turn (Lukes 1986).

The observable actualities of non-decision-making power in conservation closely match the perceptions professed by IMB stakeholders. Sociological studies of environmental politics describe the significant role of the public in legitimizing conservation and other environmental issues. Public environmental concern has been approached by sociologists with a variety of measures and instruments and has yielded a complex array of findings that link concern to pro-environmental policy outcomes (Dunlap 1995; Agnone 2007), describe a transformation in popular conceptions of nature itself (Buttel 1978; Dunlap

2008), examine the relationship between concern and pro-environmental behavior (Kollmuss and Agyeman 2002; Lee et al. 2014), and more. Moreover, sociologists of science describe the processes by which agenda-setting determines the scientific research that is done or not done (Frickel et al. 2010). While there has been a reasonably long-lived debate regarding whether public support for pro-environmental initiatives translates through the greater social structure of politics, economy, and civil society toward eventual pro-environmental results (Harrington et al. 2004), these discussions rely on more nuanced investigation of interfering forces than a conception of public support as lacking power and import. The ideal-type democratic system described by IMB stakeholders above may not perfectly operate as such, but it appears to function in a roundabout and messy way to legitimize conservation action with popular support.

Decision-making power in species conservation is not always the collaborative process that it is frequently perceived to be, especially at critical junctures. Evidence of this fact can be found in accounts of the IMB's conservation history. A salient example of decision-making power in IMB conservation is the FWS decision to respond to the 2002 Xerces Society petition to list the IMB as endangered under the ESA by precluding the butterfly from listing. It is not an exaggeration to say that the great majority of IMB stakeholders interviewed either did not know or declined to mention that this decision was not collectively made within the FWS. Indeed, several key IMB stakeholders expressed confusion and frustration regarding the decision, explaining that they still did not know how it had come to pass. Those who were both close to the decision at the time and who also expressed disagreement with its outcome described a process by which a single individual disrupted what was meant to be a collective decision-making process. One NGO worker, William, recounted the events:

> Ultimately the U.S. Fish and Wildlife Service did not—as you know— did not list it, even though their biologists felt that it should be listed. [...] Basically, the U.S. Fish and Wildlife Service did a positive 90-day finding, and then reversed that in the last few months before it was released. They reversed it at the request of [*redacted*], who was the [*redacted*] of the U.S. Fish and Wildlife Service. [...] And this is not an isolated incident of agency scientists—U.S. Fish and Wildlife Service scientists—finding that an animal should be protected or should have a certain amount of critical habitat, and then the agency basically overrules their own scientists and makes the opposite decision. Um. Not at all uncommon.

As William indicates, though the decision was in part collective, it was ultimately, utterly individual. Moreover, being that the decision was in disagreement with agency scientists' consensus, it directly contradicts the aforementioned stakeholder who described the legal nuances by which listing decisions must rely on available science. While the motivations of the individual in question remain unclear, it is widely reported among stakeholders that the decision not to list the IMB was not supported by the scientists investigating the butterfly.

The individual who exerted agency to block the ESA decision is one in a chain of possible individuals who could have done so as the ESA listing decision approached the Deputy Director of the U.S. Department of the Interior (DOI). The actuality of ESA listing decisions is that while they are commonly imagined as being collective decisions based on best available science, collectively derived agendas are ultimately bottlenecked into moments of individual decision-making. Indeed, it is not simply a matter of trickle-down political culture that Democratic presidents tend to pass more ESA listings than Republican presidents (Czech and Krausman 2001); it is the design of the governmental apparatus that executives and their appointed cabinets can, if they desire for any reason, delay ESA listings or halt them entirely. Significantly, however, it is worth noting that the negative ESA decision was rapidly met with a lawsuit on behalf of the Xerces Society. Checks and balances on individual decision-making power exist for this very reason, though in urgent cases of species extinction, they may not have time to function as intended before irreparable loss results.

In further examples of individual decision-making power despite perceptions of collectivity, the NPS at American Camp exhibits in its history a few key choices. In particular, the director of NPS at the time of the IMB's discovery and subsequent conservation action was referenced widely in stakeholder interviews as having made rogue decisions on key issues. In particular, the individual committed to use of herbicides at American Camp without consulting other IMB stakeholders. Additionally, this NPS director took rogue exterminatory actions against the rabbit population of American Camp. Unlike the unfavorable listing decision, stakeholders did not necessarily express disagreement (though some did vehemently disagree) with these choices, only the decision-making power that was seized by a single individual in their implementation. The NPS director in question ultimately left and/or was removed from their position. Further, a part of the community of San Juan Island formed a "S.O.B." or "Save Our Bunnies" campaign, which protested in Friday Harbor. This community backlash has led to a stalemate on park decision-making regarding the American Camp rabbit population (that persists today) and is thus a further example of checks on individual decision-making power. Still, it is undeniable that the individual in question, having singly held and wielded the power to assign the right to life and death among the species of American Camp, further exhibited that decision-making power in many ways ultimately falls on single persons. Further examples of this (and less destructive examples) in the IMB's history include: the initial inception of a captive-rearing program by a single individual; the commitment of other individuals to centering dissertations and theses on IMB research, resulting in a vital windfall of IMB science; and the day-to-day decisions made by the NPS workers who operate the captive rearing lab to, with delicacy and care, release eclosed butterflies so that they will have the best chance at survival.

To understand this phenomenon of the perception of decision-making power as residing among the collective despite the especially significant role individual decisions have played in IMB conservation, I turn to Weber's (and similarly though distinctly used by Arendt) conceptual distinction between *force* and *authority* (Spencer 1970; Arendt 1970). For Weber, power exists as a duality on a continuum of social legitimacy, ranging from violent, coercive *force* to subversive, collective *authority* (Spencer 1970). By this theory, the individually made decisions described above vary from the collective decision-making commonly described by IMB stakeholders in that these moments are exactions of force rather than authority. This speaks to the nature of both force and authority in IMB conservation. The fact that most individuals involved in IMB conservation express ignorance regarding the individualized application of force exacted in the 2006 negative ESA decision evidences the perceived absence of force, despite its quite salient historical role. An accounting of IMB conservation as a matter of individuals and force runs counter to the commonly shared belief that the enterprise is steered collectively. Alternatively, the nature of authority in IMB conservation reveals the function of legitimacy in normalizing collectively made decisions, maintaining the myth of their singular influence. This conception of authority accounts, for example, for the difference between rogue herbicide application or rabbit extermination and the application of controlled prairie burns, butterfly mark-release-recapture, soil disturbance, and other actions that observably manipulate the ecosystem at American Camp and beyond. In sum, authority in IMB conservation serves to determine which decisions are or are not incorporated into the IMB's popular history, a process by which stakeholders develop a common description of power that does not match the historical actuality of its enforcement.

Understanding the function and nature of ideological power in species conservation is one topic wherein conservation science can be especially enhanced by wider reading and incorporation of environmental sociological theory and research (thus developing a conservation sociology). Moreover, it is one issue by which the most concrete connections might be made visible between the global context of sociopolitical inertia toward abating environmental degradation and biodiversity loss to the local context of IMB conservation in the San Juan Islands. To guide this discussion, a question: In the era of least ESA listings since the law's inception, why has the IMB been successfully listed?

In response, I offer several relevant findings from related research. The IMB persists in and around a community which exhibits several qualities linked to positive municipal conservation outcomes: high liberal politicization, high wealth, high conservation ethos, high education, a growing eco-tourist industry, an established conservation infrastructure, and an absence of social groups in conditional opposition to conservation goals (Kellert 1985; Forester and Machlis 1996; Doremus 1997; Czech et al. 1998; Ando 1999; Langpap and Kerkvliet 2010; Puckett et al. 2016). From a perspective wrought from these collective findings, ESA listing decisions do, in actuality, very much appear to take into account social factors as much as scientific ones. To take a classic example, was the Spotted Owl ultimately protected at the direct expense of Northern California's timber industry? Or, was the owl's listing made structurally viable by a trend of global divestment from American timber in support of Canadian, Indian, and other growing timber industries? In the IMB's case we might ask similar questions and find answers that indicate the positive relationships between expensive housing markets, municipal environmental maintenance, and the health of eco-tourism industries. This work cannot with its limited data sources explicate in real terms this chain of interconnected socio-economic parts operating in conjunction with successful IMB listing and conservation. Yet, these data do warrant articulation that those most closely monitoring and laboring on the IMB conservation effort do not profess attention to these vital social variables, which may indeed be most responsible for the IMB's skirting of extinction. In sociological research of conservation, we draw from the collectivity of findings an indication that if a species' federal legal protection directly interferes with capitalist machinations, it is perhaps less likely to be listed endangered. Conversely, in cases such as the IMB's in which the species conservation is aligned with the local machinations of capitalism (i.e., eco-tourism, expensive housing), an endangered species—particularly perhaps one so romantic as a butterfly—can perhaps become a kind of commodity.

Though further research is required to investigate this phenomenon in species conservation, similar patterns can be found elsewhere in socioenvironmental action and discourse. In the popular Western discourse surrounding climate change, for example, authority and hegemony legitimize a suggestion that science, if it allows market forces to instrumentalize it, will develop in ever-climbing spiral patterns of technological advancement and consequent profit, an "ecological modernization" culminating in the abolishment of environmental degradation (Mol et al. 2009). Billionaires are lauded for contributing hearty donations toward technocratic solutions that simultaneously widen the gap between rich and poor, while grassroots activists like Greta Thunberg, Bill McKibben, and others are tolerated up to the point that they begin openly implicating the political-economic apparatus (Caldwell 2019). Beyond the environmental movement, this trend extends in a roughly similar fashion to the civil rights, animal rights, peace, and other counterculture social movements. Famously, Martin Luther King Jr.'s final speech before his assassination was explicitly anti-capitalist, his proposed solutions to racial problems directly challenging a dominant political-economic ideology that persists today in the bifurcated form of neoconservativism and neoliberalism.

Sociological theory suggests that, existing as a matter of civil society, conservation is likely to operate in some form as a hegemonic mechanism. The social processes that select desirable species for tokenized protection, without acknowledging or addressing underlying causes of biodiversity loss, will not prevent a broader ecological collapse and do not appear to be designed to address or even acknowledge the underlying causes necessary to do so. It can least be the imperative of serious conservation actors to settle for protecting species on behalf of affluent communities, to give space to ecology only when it is socially convenient, and to deny species the right to life where they disrupt the progress of the bulldozers of industrial capitalism. As one government employee, Lauren, said to me of the IMB:

> I think it comes to a point for me personally where I wanna know at what point are we intervening beyond what would be naturally appropriate? I personally struggle with how long will captive rearing be done and to what, you know, are we crossing a threshold where now we are manufacturing butterflies and planting butterfly gardens for our own edification? So the 'why' for me—I am not a biologist. I don't— there's a lot of questions that I have from a rudimentary level about what we're doing and why we're doing it.

For Lauren, who works very closely with IMB conservation, it is not clear that IMB conservation is a purely pro-ecological enterprise lacking ulterior motives and consequences. Indeed, to write honestly, a part of the ethnographic experience of studying IMB conservation was coming to wonder, despite the great earnestness, intelligence, and passion of IMB advocates, whether there was not something disingenuous buried underneath the grand collective endeavor to protect the butterfly. Conservation science and practice, when component parts of capitalism, serve to contain, limit, and control environmental protections. To paraphrase the stakeholder above, is the goal of conservation ecological health, or is it human control over ecology? In the neoliberal capitalist context, I would argue it does appear the latter, as alarm bells sound loudest when wild ecology either threatens to grow disruptively, or, in the case of the IMB of the San Juan Islands, threatens to recede without human consent. Consider the congruency, for example, between the protection of a butterfly on NPS land in an affluent eco-tourism destination and the social context in which Jeff Bezos, Amazon.com Inc. founder and wealthiest person alive, can ostensibly assert his climate activism on the basis of his placing $10 billion within his own "Earth Fund," and Bill Gates, fourth wealthiest person alive, can author a book about preventing climate disaster without reflection on the gross incongruency of his social position relative to the causes of climate change (Gamboa 2021; Gates 2021). From this theoretical perspective, one might understand these actions as motivated by power and control over urgent social movements that may otherwise determine radical solutions, rather than altruistic philanthropy.

Finally, it is worth supplementing this discussion with a brief account of the ostracization of indigenous communities from IMB conservation. There now exists a substantial collection of social scientific research on species conservation documenting not only the high value of indigenous culture and knowledge to localized conservation efforts but the inseparability of the legacy of colonialism from contemporary social processes resulting in biodiversity loss (Gadgil et al. 1993; Kimmerer 2013; Ban et al. 2018; Artelle et al. 2019). In the contemporary conservation context, no conservation collaboration can be said to be following best practices without consulting local indigenous leaders and experts. In the case of the IMB, I witnessed no evidence that any attempt had been made at any time to incorporate these resources (though it is possible an effort existed without my knowledge or has existed since 2018, when this research was conducted). Two interview participants, from a predominately white sample, expressed emotions ranging from concern to dismay over this exclusion.

From a sociological perspective, the exclusion of indigenous peoples from IMB conservation is non-random and intimately related to the power dynamics described in this chapter. The San Juan Islands have been inhabited by humans for 6,000-8,000 years. In pre-colonial times, the area was inhabited by six to eight tribes including the Saanich, Songhee, Lummi, Samish, Sooke, and Semiahmoo (NPS 2021). These people employed fishing, agricultural, and seasonal migration technologies that, prior to the introduction of and replacement by the technologies of colonial capitalism, were far less harmful to local ecology than current social systems (ibid.). European diseases introduced in the late 1700's decimated local indigenous populations. Eventually, the U.S. government claimed the islands and began a settler homesteading project. Now, this legacy of homesteading dominates the culture and ethos of the San Juan Islands, and the multi-millennia legacy of indigenous peoples is practically invisible except when driving through the Swinomish Reservation to get to Anacortes from Seattle. Indigenous perspectives, as outsiders even to the non-decision-making processes of power, may be critical of the neoliberal hegemony of contemporary American conservation. To implement indigenous perspectives into a conservation collaboration is to implement questions about the relationship between extinction and capitalism, white supremacy, classism, and colonialism. Consequently, even in a context of high environmental concern and the unlikely successful listing of an unassuming butterfly under the ESA during an anti-environmental political regime, the power dynamics that traverse macro-level social structures of political economy down to local conservation governance render the critical perspectives of indigenous peoples as subaltern, even at the expense of conservation knowledge and practice. Moreover, for as long as conservationism is undergirded by the hegemony of neoliberalism, the very suggestion that an alternative ideology take meaningful part in a conservation collaboration threatens the authority of a political-economic system that is openly engaging in mass species extinction as a default process of its exploitation of ecology.

Conclusion

Data gathered from interviews with IMB stakeholders amounts to an illustration of the perceptions of power popularly held among this conservation community. Relying on sociological theories of power to parse facets of power and, in particular, to make intelligible a diffuse ideological power, these perceptions of facets of power are compared with "actualities" assembled from contemporary theory and research. The ensuing disparities between the perception and actuality of decision-making and ideological powers do not conflict with most existing research. Rather, perceptions of decision-making power reflect expectations that designed mechanisms of collective decision-making will function properly, while incidents of individual co-optation of collective decision-making, having positive and negative conservation impacts, occur more commonly than acknowledged. And, perceptions of ideological power reflect the very operation of ideological power, as contemporary political-economic structures are rendered as immutable and natural, despite these structures being the underlying causes of species endangerment and therefore necessary to change in order to achieve the stated goal of species conservation. Yet, in the Actualities of Power section I argue that the IMB's particular context provides an opportunity for tokenized protection of the butterfly within a capitalist, neoliberal political-economic system, due in particular to the affluence, environmental ethic, and growing ecotourism industry of the San Juan Islands. The result is a rendering of social power in the microcosm of IMB conservation, as well as a nesting of power in IMB conservation among a greater political-economic context, helping us to understand why the IMB is among the only species to acheive an ESA listed status under the Trump administration.

In describing ideological power, I put forth arguments that neoliberalized species conservation does not appear to address the underlying causes of biodiversity loss. These conversations are significantly more common in sociological subfields related to the environment and animals than they are in conservation biology. I would like to suggest that having these discussions in mainstream conservation science is both urgent and necessary. As research continues to cast doubt over whether providing greater information or incentives to the public leads to informed related policy outcomes (an indictment of the ideological function of perceived human rationality), it is time for scientists, both natural and social, to turn away from individualizing responsibility for environmental solutions and turn toward addressing underlying structural causes and developing systemic policy solutions. For the IMB, perhaps the causal direction of the popular "butterfly effect" is reversed: extant large-scale conditions are set in motion a deterministic non-linear system that may stop the butterfly's wings from flapping, or, perhaps more perversely, simply make for it its wings to flap as decoration.

Chapter 5

Problems of Time: Describing Temporal Obstacles to Species Conservation at the Intersection of Society and Ecology

It is a May afternoon in the San Juan Islands, and I am waiting to be contacted by a biological technician seasonally employed with the National Park Service (NPS). Each Island Marble Butterfly (IMB) at the American Camp National Park captive rearing lab will transform and emerge on its own time, but today we are in luck. A butterfly has eclosed from its chrysalis, one of the first of the season, and I rush to the park to watch its release. At first, it is not clear whether the clouds queuing in staggered traffic overhead will break, but by the time we are in the field, time and space have unfolded on the prairie into a moment confluent with clarity and sunshine. We waste no time clambering through tall weeds, and soon my guide stops, opens the container, and slowly, patiently urges the neophyte butterfly into the world. I snap dozens of photos, preserving a flipbook of consecutive instants in flat, rectangular cross-sections. We want it to take flight, but the butterfly takes its time. We wait, watching the sun warm its wings, and after a moment it flutters up, then collapses deep into the brush. The biological technician locates it and carefully clears a path upward. When the butterfly alights again, we are satisfied that it will, with time, settle into its natural freedoms. It will fly for at most a week or so before it will die. For me, the moment stretches on far beyond, carried in memory to recall later, here. The urgency, the waiting, the fortune and chance of misfortune, the butterfly on its own time and me on my own, I think all of it belies a ubiquitous common ground, a dimensional axis shared by individuals, societies and ecologies, something that undergirds every happening and mishappening: time.

Time, in its scarcity and abundance, swiftness and sluggishness, clock-bound cycles and infinite linear expanse, is experienced relatively by perspective and context. As Einstein observed, time is everywhere there is mass, and everywhere there is variation in mass, time is relative (Robinson 1990). It exists through the movement and change of the physical and social worlds, embedded in the ubiquitous and persistent transformation of space. Where time's plurality juxtaposes against itself, we sometimes find disruptions to our social and biophysical schedules. Depending on when, what, and where we are, we may find ourselves slow or fast, early or late, urgent or leisurely, young or old, inexperienced or experienced, caterpillars or butterflies. This chapter describes an ontological framework for interpreting characteristics of these "problems of time" (as they will be called here) in the practice of species conservation, extracting perceived problems of time from the accounts of stakeholders in the case of the Island Marble Butterfly. A framework for describing and interpreting problems of time is developed by applying a critical realist ontology to matters of time in a socio-biophysical context. This framework advances theoretical descriptions of time in environmental sociology and also provides a model for applied use in identifying, describing, and finding solutions to problems of socioenvironmental time in species conservation. In other words, by beginning at a theoretical point of interpreting the sociocultural components of time as equally real, observable, and describable as the biophysical components of time, I will draw attention to the usefulness of identifying and potentially addressing socio-biophysical "problems of time" in species conservation.

This research chapter is motivated by a pattern in the interview data of stakeholders raising concern over a wide variety of conservation issues related to social and biophysical time. The analysis seeks to understand the consistencies between these disparate issues, as well as the broader disjuncture, if one should be exhibited, between social time and biophysical time. The analysis thus directed, findings indicate that stakeholders broadly and thoroughly recognize a number of such temporal issues in IMB conservation. However, depending on whether these issues are in nature social, biophysical, or somewhere between, they receive different subsequent treatment as component factors of the conservation effort. Consequently, this chapter seeks to render visible these factors, describe them, and to suggest pathways forward for IMB conservation to address social and biophysical "problems of time" alike.

Conceptualizing Socio-biophysical Time

While it is often written that time is understudied by sociologists, it is also often observed by social scientists of time that its study is in actuality quite pervasive, being an implicit component of most any kind of social theory (Hassard 1990; Bergmann 1992). Indeed, sociological theorists have a fair history of including specified discussions of time in their theory-building works, or of eventually adding a text solely addressing the issue of time to a body of interrelated theory. To take perhaps the original and most foundational example, as Durkheim first described "social facts" (essentially phenomena derived not from nature or human consciousness but rather the sum of social interactions), one such fact was the existence of social "rhythms," the ways in which time manifests through society in partial abstraction from individuals and biophysical processes. This essential ontological distinction that a social thing has, as Durkheim writes, "an existence of its own, independent of its individual manifestations," remains a fundamental ontological assumption that defines sociology's distinctions from other sciences (Durkheim 1982: 27). That is, as has been discussed elsewhere in this book, sociologists observe the existence of a *social* reality, as real as biophysical reality, a sort of nature of existence through which forces exist independently of individuals' consciousness and biophysical objects (though these realities may influence one another). Durkheim advanced this philosophical point in order to enhance science's ability to detect and investigate social phenomena. For example, motivated to empirically describe the causes of suicide, Durkheim famously found individualized characteristics to be insufficient explanatory factors and so turned to the greater explanatory power of constructing theories of the influence of broader social factors on population groups (i.e., cultural and structural factors) (Durkheim 1951). The same has remained true for sociologists of time: while individuals' experiences of time as well as the biophysical realities of time are both quite relevant, to understand the machinations of time in society, one must also conceive of time in its uniquely social reality.

Since Durkheim, time has been treated by a great many sociological theorists. Perhaps the most influential work in the American context is Pitirim Sorokin and Robert Merton's 1937 *American Journal of Sociology* article, in which they offer the first real concerted effort to realize in theory time's existence as a *social fact* (Bergmann 1992). Sorokin further expanded on this theory by attempting to describe causality in terms of time in a book-length treatise in which he also makes distinctions between disciplinary conceptions of time, as Bergmann describes quoting Sorokin, emphasizing "that the social sciences are not served by a physical, mathematical, biological or psychological time, but rather need an 'adequate conception of sociocultural time as one of their main referential principles'" (Sorokin 1943, Bergmann 1992: 85). French sociologists Georges Gurvitch (1964, 1973), who penned another book-length treatise on time, and Pierre Bourdieu (1963, 1968), who incorporated chapters on time into some of his lesser read works, applied and expanded on Durkheim's perspective (Bergmann 1992). American sociologist George Herbert Mead attempted to construct a theory of time in the tradition of symbolic interactionism, the theoretical project of the so-called "Chicago School" of sociology, in which he conceived of time as being emergently generated through social action (Mead 1932). For Mead, both temporal and social realities are realized only simultaneously and only in conjunction with one another, with the "social" playing an anchoring role similar to mass in Einstein's theories of relativity (if one may draw the comparison) (ibid.).

Mead's theory has not been widely used or expanded upon (Bergmann 1992). However, its attention to understanding the nature of social reality, of the present, and of the past are mirrored in the contemporary discourse. Austrian philosopher Alfred Schutz presented a very similar and more widely applied theory of time, also explaining the emergence of time and the social as concurrent through action, which like a proverbial tree falling soundlessly in the woods, only gains meaningful existence once it has been recognized by individuals in the context of other social things (1973). Similar to Durkheim's social *rhythms*, Schutz described an aggregation of socio-temporal events toward a socially constructed shared concept of timekeeping, which he called *world time*, and he sought beyond Durkheim's efforts to theorize greater detail of its social mechanics and components (Bergmann 1992).

In more recent decades, the project of defining and describing social time evolved into a quest for greater clarity and detail, being approached with a variety of organizational constructs and systems of concepts that require considerable discussion to parse the nuanced overlaps and distinctions within and between. Here is a brief overview guided by Hassard's review of the sociology of time (1990). Jaques tackles the philosophical questions of social time, distinguishing *chronos*, or clock-time, from *krainos*, or lived existential time, in order to argue that our inability to firmly grasp the distinction underlies essential flaws in existing social theory (1982). Gurvitch's eightfold typology of time, which includes concepts like *alternating-time*, *explosive-time*, *cyclical-time*, etc., became a point of reference for sociologists of time to begin applying and editing more descriptive models of social time (1964). Diamant (1970), deGrazia (1974), and Zerubavel (1981) treat the issue of *linear* vs. *circular* or *cyclical* time. Zerubavel also distinguished *private-time* from *public-time*, using his theory in applied studies of time in hospitals. Thompson (1967), Thrift (1983), Nyland (1990), Nowotny (1992) and others developed a theory tying social time inextricably to the material and ideological processes of capitalism, discussing how it is commoditized, unequally distributed, gendered, etc. Urry considers the role of the "future" in shaping the present organization of society (2016). In more recent years the project has flourished into a stage of broad and various application (in which this project participates), wherein scholars have theorized about the relationship between time and contemporary technology (Wajcman 2008), time and gender (Adam 2002), time and the natural environment (Cifri and Trako 2010), and much more.

Furthermore, much sociological work has been generated that is *about time* in a practical sense, having a temporal issue as the focus of empirical inquiry, rather than theory building. Perhaps the greatest impetus for this kind of research has been understanding time as it relates to work and organizations, the pace, timing, and longevity of labor hours being an extremely significant component of labor rights dating to Robert Owen's (ca. 1810) championship of an eight-hour work week (Cahill 2007). Hassard (1999), Perlow (1997), Postone (1993) and more have developed a rich body of research on the role of time in organizing labor, often applying theories of time and capitalism. Further, scholars of historical sociology have treated the central role of time in their broader query (Aminzade 1992; Isaac 1997). More recently, an attention to the ordering and timing of events in one's life has given rise to a body of "life course" literature in sociology, which considers outcomes related to issues such as physical and mental health, achievement, interpersonal relationships, etc. (Elder et al. 2003; Mayer 2009). Age, aging, and generationality have also been the subject of considerable sociological scholarship (Settersten and Angel 2011; Leonard 2016), and such "generations" and their distinctions are among the most widely and commonly discussed sociological concepts present in the discourse of popular American media.

For the purpose of brevity, we might organize the empirical frameworks regarding social time into two broadly composed traditions: that of the positivistic and Functionalist framers who seek to describe the mechanisms by which modern societies manifest "temporal order," time-keeping, scheduling, and collective rhythm; and, that of the conflict- and positional-oriented, who draw attention to the pluralities of social time and its function as a tool of power. This work follows in the second tradition for two reasons. First, the pluralist tradition is congruent with the theoretical approaches underlying this total manuscript. Second, being motivated by a pro-biodiversity ethic to attend to obstacles to species conservation (as a work of conservation sociology), the focus here on "problems of time" in these endeavors is incompatible with theoretical frameworks designed to describe "temporal order" (Zerubavel 1981). As Zerubavel concedes of his theoretical perspective put forth in *Hidden Rhythms*,

> Certainly not all social life is temporally structured in a rigid manner. There are a lot of people who conduct their everyday life without using calendars and schedules, wearing a watch, or respecting deadlines, who are often late to appointments, and who sometimes forget what day it is. I am by no means oblivious to all of the above. On the contrary, I deliberately try to ignore them, for heuristic purposes. (Pg.4)

The goal here is quite the opposite: to reveal, characterize, and contextualize those exceptions to socio-temporal order, which, occurring non-randomly in quality, frequency, and position, amount to patterns of social dysfunction, conflict, and inequality. I do not imagine that anyone forgets what day it is or is late to an appointment by pure chance, but rather that the chances of these temporal disruptions occurring is mediated by a great many sociological variables. Indeed, one would not trace the late or early eclose of a butterfly to some abstract mathematical chaos, but rather seek to understand the biophysical factors that led to the disruption. In the environmental sociological study of issues related to conservation, the same empiricism one applies to the biophysical qualities of time must also be applied to the social.

For environmental sociologists, the schisms of social and natural time are embedded in our core theory. Foster's theory of metabolic rift (drawn from Marx), for example, relies on the essential idea that perpetual natural resource extraction and waste creation sum toward, with time, the "contradictions of capitalism" by which its essential processes lead to its systemic collapse (Foster 1999). In this equation, time is an essential variable. When we speak of deforestation, biodiversity loss, climate change, or other major environmental calamities, we often measure their urgency by the disjuncture in *rate* between how quickly human systems are transforming biophysical systems and how quickly biophysical systems can recover through natural processes. Indeed, biodiversity loss may be conceived of as a kind of "problem of time" between human social and biophysical time scales, extinction being an inevitable eventuality on a geological time scale, but its current accelerated rate yielding dramatic, unnatural effects. Conservation, temporally speaking, is taking action to slow down an extinction rate.[1] This conception also undergirds major environmental sociological ideas like the "Treadmill of Production" (Gould et al. 2008), which describes the structural processes by which metabolic rifts accelerate over time, or its converse, "Ecological Modernization Theory," which asserts that metabolic rifts can decelerate over time (Mol et al. 2009). Acknowledgement that social time and biophysical time are distinct yet crucially interrelated is one of the fundamental facts of environmental sociology.

Beyond an implicit presence in theory, time has only rarely and recently been an object of inquiry for environmental sociologists, and almost not at all by Americans, much of the work remaining yet untranslated to English. Separately, Geissler (1993), Held (1993), and Kümmerer (1993) began the conversation with theoretical reflections on time and the environment nested in contributions from the sociology of time, which is continued in a similar fashion by Rager (2001), Reheis (2009), and Cifri (2010). In brief, these works articulate with various nomenclature an abstract distinction between social time and biophysical time, which is precisely the idea that I am hoping to demonstrate in an applied context here. Shove et al. (2009) and Schor (1998)

---

[1] Alternatively, these environmental crises may be conceived of as instances of what Urry calls "Cassandra Syndrome," which are moments in which commonly shared observations of future calamities arise but the calamities are yet unable to be stopped (2016).

touch lightly on time and environment but do so in the context of work and everyday life. Cifri and Trako trace the root of socioenvironmental problems to the historical transformation of dominant conceptions of social time as cyclical toward conceptions of time as linear (2010), a theory also mirrored in the writings of Stephen Jay Gould (1987), who was especially interested in geological time. This thesis is too broad and abstract to directly apply to the case of the IMB here, but as results are presented, readers are encouraged to attend to the quite apparent discrepancies between the linear nature of social time and the cyclical nature of biophysical time. These theories of time and environment have not yet been applied to empirical research, and much more work is needed to tether them to observable reality and to prove what scientific usefulness they may offer. Let this chapter be a small movement in this direction.

Having established a review of the theoretical treatment of time and environment in sociology and environmental sociology, the chapter now turns to a brief philosophical discussion of the issue, which will yield the ontological framework through which will be interpreted "problems of time" as having distinct social and biophysical realities. To this end, the chapter here employs a Bhaskarian critical realist framework, which is characterized by an overlapping dual reality of the sociocultural and the biophysical (Bhaskar 2005). At the point of overlap, these two realms form a socio-biophysical reality. In essence, critical realism is a philosophy of science that reconciles the ontological perspectives (that is, perspectives about what is real, the nature of existence, and how things come to exist) of the natural and social sciences by, to put it simply, claiming that both natural and social things have realities, and these realities co-exist in a shared socio-biophysical realm that encompasses most observable things. Most any object or idea one can conjure will have both a natural, material existence and a social, cultural existence, both simultaneously real. As Carolan points out in his seminal work on the socio-biophysical existence of "nature," such an ontological perspective is especially useful to scholars of environmental sociology, as it gives language to the ontological assumption of a dual socioenvironmental reality underlying their discipline (2005). This Bhaskarian critical realism has since been applied to the study of various environmental phenomena, developing ontologies of climate change (Esbjörn-Hargens 2010), sustainability (York and Clark 2010), the GMO controversy (Carolan 2008), and more.

While Carolan uses Bhaskar's critical realism to dissect the existence of nature, dividing it into "nature" (sociocultural), nature (socio-biophysical), and Nature (biophysical), the framework is here used to interpret time in the context of nature(s). That is, the framework is used for interpreting nature in particular because this analysis is investigating nature as well, only in its temporal form, as a kind of nature-time. In the sociocultural realm where Carolan places the discursive elements of what is deemed natural and the dynamics of power invested therein, here is being supplemented the associated processes of time, such as those theories described above that emphasize the un-"natural"ness of socially constructed time. In the biophysical category, the realm of "deep strata" of "gravity, thermodynamics, ecosystem processes that we have yet to grasp" (Carolan 2005: 406), here is being supplemented the physics of time and the unknown temporal qualities of ecology. Lastly, in the socio-biophysical realm belongs everything else that has temporal existence: clocks and hours, weeks and seasons, years and ages, urgency, leisure, schedules, calendars, etc. Important to note is that these triplicate categories are not exclusive, nor does any category manifest anything "purely." In fact, as Carolan points out, when one looks deep enough at the "purely" sociocultural or biophysical, they will find components of the other therein, or at least they will find that these "deep" realms are in some state of perpetual change and relativity. Moreover, they shape one another reciprocally (Carolan 2005).

So, the framework employed by this chapter uses Bhaskar's critical realism to lay overlapping triplicate categorizations onto problems of time found in interviews and ethnography related to IMB conservation. In doing so, we are able to legitimize such socio-biophysical problems of time as objects of consideration, assess their characteristics using social theory, and develop patterns in the data that reveal how ontological quality may affect a problem of time's perception or solvability. In grounding these theories in a real-world case study, we confront not only the socio-biophysical realities underlying each problem of time, but also the variation in human perception that renders part (either social or biophysical) of any such problem invisible or visible to some. Especially, the analysis will indicate that while many "problems of time" in IMB conservation, being socio-biophysical phenomena, have both sociocultural and biophysical components, the biophysical aspects are often treated as more solvable, scientific, and relevant to conservation. IMB stakeholders identify the sociocultural components of many problems of time, but this identification does not appear to frequently translate into conservation action, as they instead tend to favor describing and working toward solutions to the biophysical components. Figure 5.1 outlines this critical realist ontology and provides general examples.

Figure 5.1. Critical Realist Ontology of Time with Selected Examples

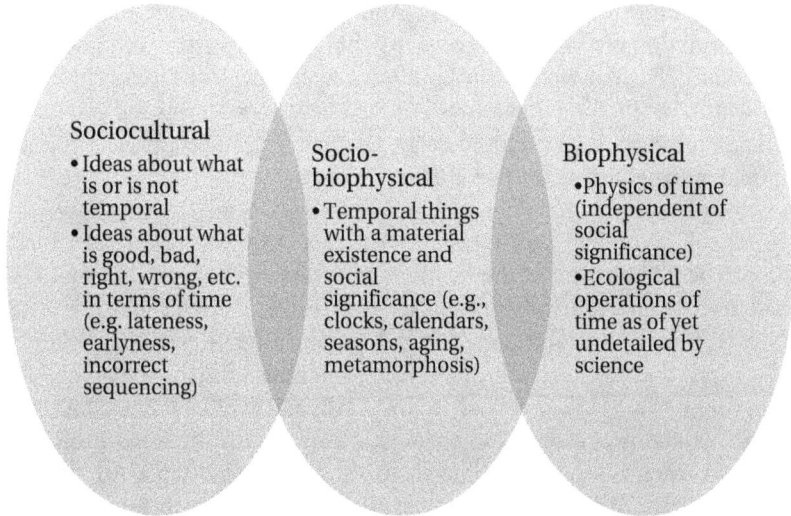

Sociocultural
- Ideas about what is or is not temporal
- Ideas about what is good, bad, right, wrong, etc. in terms of time (e.g. lateness, earlyness, incorrect sequencing)

Socio-biophysical
- Temporal things with a material existence and social significance (e.g., clocks, calendars, seasons, aging, metamorphosis)

Biophysical
- Physics of time (independent of social significance)
- Ecological operations of time as of yet undetailed by science

At this point, this piece will theorize time and environment no further, seeking instead to discuss in-depth the role of time in generating obstacles to IMB conservation. However, in doing so, the analysis will lay out evidence in support of a central thesis of this chapter: the sociological conception of time is ontologically unique, and explicit identification and description of sociological "problems of time" in species conservation yields a fresh imagination of obstacles to conservation goals, rendering also fresh solutions. In other words, the analysis is using theory to develop a versatile heuristic of social time in environmental issues, which will position conservation actors to make a variety of tangible, practical applications in research, employment, fieldwork, outreach, policy, and other social components of species conservation work. Thus, the chapter is imagined to provide an example of the kinds of active prescriptions for applied conservation work that may emerge from a conservation sociology.

Problems of Time in IMB Conservation

I met an IMB conservation stakeholder, Carol, on San Juan Island for an interview in her garden, which was wild, diverse, and teeming with plant and animal life. Carol had been living on the island for a few decades, and as she surveyed her property, she reflected on her vantage on the passage of time:

> I moved here when I was just thirty years old, and I never thought I would live to see a fir tree grow from (*laughing*) *this* big to *that*. And it's

put an entirely different perspective on life, because now I really see how things change constantly. And there's a constant rhythm of... Bumm. Bumm. I mean some of the madrone trees that were so beautiful when we moved here have aged and lost limbs. I thought within my lifetime that tree was gonna be the way it was for, you know, one hundred, two hundred years. So there's an awareness as you get older (*laughing*) that there is constant change.

For Carol, aging had transformed her perspective on the rate at which the biophysical landscape of the San Juan Islands had changed, but that change had also been real and observable, the result of time's passage through cyclical biophysical and sociocultural processes. The San Juan Islands are changing and so too are the ecological and human social conditions governing the IMB's survival. Many IMB stakeholders described shared concerns about obstacles to conservation relating to time, and this section presents each of these "problems of time" in turn. Table 5.1 provides a reference list of the problems discussed here. As problems of time are described, brief reflections on their sociocultural and biophysical components draw out patterns in the relationship between issues' ontology, apparent solvability, and individuals' relative positionality, which are further treated in the final sections of the chapter.

Table 5.1. Problems of Time with Associated Ontological Positions

Problem of Time	Ontological Position
Residential Turnover	More Sociocultural
Increasing Tourism	More Sociocultural
Staff Turnover	More Sociocultural
Pace of Bureaucracy	More Sociocultural
Interrelatedness of Funding and Research	More Sociocultural
Presidential Cycles	More Sociocultural
Synchronizing Collaborative Information	More Sociocultural
Seasonal Employment	Socio-biophysical
Waiting Until Listing to Conserve	Socio-biophysical
Ignorance of Butterfly Lifecycles	Socio-biophysical
Rabbit Boom/Bust Cycles	More Biophysical
Caterpillar-Host Plant De-Sync	More Biophysical

At a high level of concern are the rates of *residential turnover* and *increasing tourism* which have resulted in rapid transformation of the San Juan Islands' social composition. Ethan, a non-profit leader local to San Juan Island described the rapid turnover of local home ownership:

> Really our population turns over pretty fast. We've got this kind of core group of islanders, but, 40% of the houses in the archipelago are vacation homes [...] and are not occupied year-round. And so, you've got this kind of constant kind of influx of people from other places who are buying property here and they're relocating - in a lot of cases they don't make it through the first year. It's like, 'That's not what I thought it was going to be! I'm not really cut out for this.' So, we have this high turnover rate, and so for our organization or any organization or any issue, it's this constant kind of re-education effort you have to do. People are cycling. You get a third loss every three years or something like that. So, it's a big shift. A decade from now, 80% of the people you'd be talking to now will not necessarily be here.

Ethan argued that rapid *residential turnover* was a problem because it results in an increased demand for public outreach and reeducation, much of which remains local only for a short time. From a conservation outreach perspective, each time a new homeowner moves in, they must be educated about local wildlife safety, and each time a homeowner moves away, education has been lost from the community. This issue is particularly relevant as The Washington Department of Fish and Wildlife (WDFW) pursues a "Candidate Conservation Agreement with Assurances" strategy to enforcement of the IMB as a federally listed endangered species, a program through which state government negotiates with local landowners to establish habitats for the species on their land in exchange for legal protections against being prosecuted for accidental harm. Furthermore, many of those interviewed who make their homes on the San Juan Islands also expressed concern that rates of *residential turnover* were also transforming local culture and politics. Several participants drew connections between residential turnover and local social problems, such as a lack of affordable housing. One stakeholder, Lauren, brought up the issue of affordable housing, linking the problem to the rise of tourism:

> I keep up on local politics to some degree. (*Sighs*). [...] There's certainly a necessary push right now for affordable housing, and I think it looks like we've got a good affordable housing measure on the ballot that's gonna pass this time. Anything we can do in that regard is important for the long-term down here. And there's always a tension between the dependence of the economy on tourism and the impact

of tourism. No one on San Juan Island who lives here wants to be in Friday Harbor between July 4th and (*laughing*) Labor Day weekend.

This stakeholder described an on-going process by which *residential turnover* and *increasing tourism* were changing the composition of landowners in the islands, making housing scarcer for members of the service sector, and, in some ways, changing the lifestyles of islanders. Indeed, several stakeholders alluded to a broader cultural transformation resultant from this change. While stakeholders would rarely express personal identification with this concern, they would often locate it among long-time islanders, describing an abstract sort of worry shared among unnamed members of the community. There is some evidence of the presence of this broader concern about a culture shift on the islands: on Lopez Island, a quite popular bumper sticker reads, "Don't change Lopez. Let Lopez change you."

However, not all IMB stakeholders found *residential turnover* to be a problem, some citing what they described as a congruent ethic among old residents, new residents, and tourists alike, one of respect for the islands and concern for maintaining natural environment. This maintenance, in seeking to preserve an ever-changing biophysical environment in a state of perceived health or perfection, engages in efforts to confront problems of time that are more characterized by a biophysical existence than a sociocultural one. For example, one FWS employee (who lives and works elsewhere in Washington) described a memory in which hundreds of Douglas Fir trees had sprouted across the prairie of American Camp before NPS workers removed them, thereby preventing the prairie from transforming into the broad, shady glade of conifers that the firs, in a cyclically defined moment of expansive seed propagation, had attempted to found. Many respondents also expressed concern about the capacity for climate change to increase rates at which storm surges occur on American Camp's southern Fourth of July beach. Such storm surges threaten those IMBs who choose the tall peppergrass *Lepidium virginicum* (a native grass) as their host plant. Consequently, some stakeholders doubt its viability as a host plant on which to rely in restoring IMB populations, thus opting to support increased efforts to propagate the non-native mustards *Brassica campestris* and *Sisymbrium altissimum.* In this way, socioculturally derived judgments take aim at biophysical problems of time that disrupt collective visions of what elements of the San Juan Islands' natural environment should be preserved or should be allowed to change.

Maintenance of the San Juan Islands' natural environment has helped develop a boom in local eco-tourism. Running on fixed cyclical schedules (though frequently running late), ferries move among the islands, periodically stopping in Friday Harbor to load and unload swarms of vacationers and day-trippers, many of them there to bike, to hike, to observe plants and animals, and likely to catch a glimpse of the local southern resident killer whales. This tourism industry is fixed partially to the biophysical by the seasonal cycles that dictate humans' tolerance for exposure to the elements, but much more so, it is a sociocultural link between the islands and the economic conditions of a broader society. Stakeholders who were islanders and many who were not described a belief that *increasing tourism* was outgrowing local community and infrastructure, expressing frustration about Friday Harbor's vehicle and pedestrian crowdedness, ferry availability for locals, and the potential risks to American Camp presented by tourists, who may trample IMBs or accidentally set wildfire. As it is catalyzed by quite broad economic and cultural forces, *increasing tourism* is largely described by IMB stakeholders a kind of aggravating inevitability. Being primarily a sociocultural problem of time and therefore lacking in practical biophysical solutions, *increasing tourism* is not for IMB stakeholders a problem that can be readily solved, despite their consistent description of the issue's relevance to IMB conservation.

This feeling of helplessness in the face of sociocultural problems of time was also exhibited especially in discussions about the rates of organizational cycles and change, especially *staff turnover, seasonal employment,* and the *pace of bureaucracy.* S*taff turnover* was identified as a problem of time especially frequently by stakeholders, who expressed frustration with the NPS in particular. NPS employees often described an organizational structure that demanded high turnover rates through a process of promotion-and-exit by which NPS workers are encouraged to trade permanent residency for career advancement. Indeed, there has apparently been near total turnover in San Juan Island NPS staff since the first major concerted conservation efforts of the late 2000s, and other governmental agencies exhibit their fair share of turnover as well. These rapid *staff turnover* rates can behave as a problem of time if collective memory is lost or resources are spent unduly on repeated training. However, not all stakeholders agree that turnover is a bad thing. As Winston, a conservationist no longer active in IMB work, pointedly reflected, "If there's someone in there who's good, then turnover is a bad thing. But if there's somebody in there who's bad, then turnover has a fifty/fifty chance of being a good thing." Yet another facet of the issue is the cumulative impact of high turnover rates on the composition of organizations over time. Many such positions are not as easily refilled as they are vacated, requiring careful recruitment and well-suited, qualified applicants. Consequently, from local NPS positions to positions with regional and national jurisdictions, from NPS to FWS and beyond, stakeholders described a decades-long progression of increasing austerity in conservation-related governmental employment. Not only are governmental conservation positions held in increasing brevity, but they are also diminishing in quantity—a phenomenon generally believed to negatively impact conservation initiatives.

Seasonal employment behaves similarly as a problem of time in its necessity for increased training (as each new employee must not only be trained but must take the time necessary for themselves to routinize and perfect their mode of operations), but for those IMB stakeholders who are seasonally employed, it can also bring uncertainty about future living and working conditions. Perhaps for this reason, only seasonally employed stakeholders identified the issue as a problem of time during the interview process, others being more removed from the sociocultural conditions in which positions are assigned seasonal termination points. Yet, *seasonal employment* is also in part a response to particular cyclical biophysical phenomena that demand a related labor, being in its own sense a kind of solution to biophysical problems of time. All seasonal employees interviewed expressed some measure of contentedness in the flexibility such work afforded them, and none failed to acknowledge that many of their seasonal tasks would be impossible to perform in the off-season. However, those who more explicitly described *seasonal employment* as a problem of time expressed serious concerns. One NPS worker, Adam, told me that he felt the problem could affect not only himself but also IMB conservation:

> I mean you're essentially terminated at the end of the season. And you have to get re-hired, and so, I don't know, it's kind of a process whereas, if you're a permanent seasonal you know—it's kind of like solidified. You don't have to get re-hired every year or deal with all that. So, that would be good, I think. That's something I would like. That would be ideal for me, and also I think ideal for the butterflies and the projects in general just to keep things more consistent and spend more time actually doing what's needing to be done than learning every year or trying to teach new people every year.

Being a problem situated quite neutrally between the sociocultural and the biophysical, *seasonal employment* is a problem that, for those close enough to its sociocultural elements to identify it, sociocultural solutions are identifiable.

Lastly, some IMB conservation stakeholders expressed high concern about the *pace of bureaucracy*, especially as it relates to producing findings under the Endangered Species Act (ESA) and the ability of government to keep up with new science. For those stakeholders positioned within government agencies (e.g., FWS, WDFW, NPS, BLM, USGS), organizational sluggishness is an inconvenient fact, but one best met with adaptation of expectation and strategy. But, for many of those positioned outside government, as with local and national-level NGOs, the "grinding process" of government by which species average 12 years from petition to listing is at the root of obstacles to IMB conservation (Puckett et al. 2016). William, who leads an NGO invested in the IMB, lamented time lost to the ESA petition process:

> I liken it to, you know—this was in 2004 and 2005—this was a patient that needed chemo. Um, but it was operable cancer. Now we're like stage 5 cancer. I think the verdict is still out whether this butterfly goes extinct, and I think it is the fault of humans. It is this inaction and inability to act that has got us to this point. And it's very disappointing, because, you know, this is an animal we could have potentially—I'm not saying, we, you know—we might have done everything right. I do want to be honest that it was still critically imperiled in 2005. We just had options.

For another NGO leader, Arthur, the problem ran far deeper than the Endangered Species Act:

> Our institutions are not flexible enough. They're not resilient enough [...] Resilience: when conditions or facts change, you can change what you do to meet the facts[...] And if you're a military organization, for everything life and death depends on your ability to make a decision in the field [...] and you've got to be on top of it in 10 minutes, [...] and as soon as you engage, it starts changing and you have to keep changing your response. Well, if you're dealing with an ecosystem, it's the same thing. As soon as we engage, everything starts changing [...] But, our environmental institutions, I think, are very rigid because they are just bureaucracies like all other bureaucracies. [...] And because [these] institutions are non-resilient, they are always lagging way behind science, way behind what we know, and finding it difficult to catch up. And often by the time they catch up with an idea, science has already moved another step.

For Arthur, attending to the pace at which sociocultural structures are able to react to changes in biophysical phenomena helps to develop solutions to these socioenvironmental problems of time. This example also speaks to the role of individuals' perspectives in rendering visible the ontological components to assemble a full image of the socio-biophysical. For those inside government, its sluggishness is immutable; for those outside government, its relationship with science, nature, and environmental crisis belies a failure of design.

Some stakeholders described problems of time related to the sequencing of events, such as the *interrelatedness of funding and research* and *waiting until listing to conserve*. The *interrelatedness of funding and research* as a problem of sequence in species conservation manifests in this manner: A species is recognized as being at risk, so conservationists submit a grant soliciting funds to further research it. Funding decisions are then made in part based on existing research that might substantiate the grant's claims to urgency. The more something is studied, the more likely it becomes that its research will be granted funding. This paradoxical sequencing can make it quite difficult to turn urgency into action in the early stages of conservation. Yet, not all stakeholders perceived this issue as more than an inconvenience, and those who did perceive it as a problem implied the best solutions were built into the process: keep researching, keep writing grants, keep funding grants, and the problem is eventually overcome. The sociocultural processes by which organizations of government, university, and NGO accumulate and allocate funds for research are of course tied in the abstract to the biophysical (i.e., studies must be conducted through particular seasons), but they are also firmly rooted in the sociocultural factors of scientific production and economic transaction.

A related issue, the problem of *waiting until listing to conserve*, was for some IMB stakeholders both quite important and readily solvable. These stakeholders perceive an institutionalized unwillingness to develop conservation action until positive ESA listing decisions are made at the federal level. They argue that the correct sequence is opposite; conservation action must begin before ESA listing. One stakeholder, Lars, related specific biophysical components of the problem to its sociocultural institutionalization, citing the legal barriers they faced in implementing vital on-the-ground conservation actions to prevent butterfly populations from dying out:

> That's getting close to functional extinction, so let's make a move. [The] state says, 'Absolutely not. We forbid it.' [...] But we said, 'If we don't do that there won't be host plants—' 'Oh no! We forbid you. You can't do that.' Next year, no mustards. Following year, no more Island Marbles.

For Lars, if conservation decisions were to respond more to biophysical realities than sociocultural norms, the typical order of operations could be readily flipped. Thus, though perhaps covertly and implicitly, the ontological quality that observers assign to such problems of time appear to influence their enthusiasm to resolve the issue as a matter of IMB conservation.

Another variety of problems of time were those related to synchronization: those issues characterized by either multiple events that should not coincide happening at once or multiple events that should coincide happening disparately. Such problems were among the most prevalently and diversely described by IMB stakeholders. Two commonly identified problems of synchronization were *presidential cycles* and the *synchronicity of collaborative information*. To the first point, the relationship between which party occupies the executive branch of U.S. government and outcomes in species conservation has been well-documented, being one of the strongest known determinant social factors predicting rates of listing (Restani and Marzluff 2002). Republican presidencies are generally associated with poorer conservation outcomes, while Democratic presidencies are associated with greater conservation outcomes (ibid.).[2] This phenomenon was far from lost on IMB stakeholders, who predominantly ascribed to themselves left-leaning political tendencies. Many stakeholders expressed deep concern about the Trump administration's environmental policies, some even wondering whether species conservation as a federal project would soon cease to exist. Others matched their concern with passionate rejection of Republican leadership. As one prominent butterfly scientist, Jeremy, put it:

> Get the fucking Republicans out! You know, pardon me, Jon, but the Republican administrations ever since—after Nixon, 'cause the Nixon administration was actually pretty good for conservation—have simply tried to oblate and diminish these values and these tools and these functions at every possible opportunity.

The problem of syncing Democratic presidencies with conservation efforts is apparent to most, but this solution is deeply sociocultural and outside the purview of a specific species conservation effort such as that of the IMB. Lacking a tangible biophysical quality, conservationists tend to omit the issue from practical discussion of conservation action, rather lamenting it as relevant but, while perhaps solvable, difficult and detached from the matter at hand.

Many IMB stakeholders expressed frustration about the capacity to *synchronize collaborative information* with other stakeholders, yet there was enormous variation in perspectives on how frequently information-sharing meetings were occurring and the challenges to setting up these meetings. Some government employees cited problems of funding for travel to the San Juan Islands for meetings, some expressed that they were not being invited to meetings that must be taking place, and others spoke of routinized and regular meetings in Friday Harbor as if they were taking place without issue. Some NGO workers also expressed feeling left out, while others acknowledged

---

[2] However, it is worth noting that Republican administrations have historically been associated with some major environmental and conservation legislation. In particular, Richard Nixon signed the Endangered Species Act into law in 1973.

they had deliberately exited participation in such meetings, finding them full of conflict and deceit.[3] Lastly, those who did not occupy leadership roles expressed general confusion and frustration about such meetings' organization, usefulness, purpose, and ability to overcome challenges of time. These individuals had generally participated in one or two meetings, and when pressed for their contents, had either forgotten or expressed never knowing the real substance. For these individuals positioned on the outside looking in, the inherent problem with such meetings is clear: if many individuals are invited, there is no time to synchronize information, and if individuals are left out, less information is synchronized. Though it is of course abstractly linked to the biophysical by the finiteness of available time, these time constraints are primarily institutional. Whether observed or unobserved, this problem of time is too deeply rooted in the sociocultural for stakeholders to easily identify solutions.

Two significant problems of synchronization in IMB conservation that pertained primarily to the biophysical were *rabbit boom/bust cycles* and *caterpillar-host plant de-synchronization*. Like American presidencies, rabbit population levels on the San Juan Islands are notoriously cyclical. Long-time residents speak of an era peaking decades ago, at which point rabbits were everywhere. One young Island Marble conservationist, Kelly, who was a third-generation islander described her family's memory, "In like the 60's and 70's they were all over the whole island and you couldn't have a garden. You couldn't grow anything outside. There were roadkill on all the roads when my Mom was growing up." Once the population explodes, the rabbits face both disease and starvation. As one ecologist, Marcia, put it: "I can tell you that when the rabbit population is high enough, they will eat the death camas. I'm sure every rabbit that eats the death camas dies, but if there's enough rabbits that are each taking a bite of it, that's enough."

In more recent memory, the rabbit population has had a second decline and recovery cycle, and while the current rabbit levels are still seen as a problem in IMB conservation by many, others express contentedness at their relative scarcity and isolation to American Camp. I can personally attest that were the butterfly to return to Lopez Island today (or at least in 2018 when this research was conducted), it would face a rabbit problem comparable to San Juan Island in the 1970s; if one stands today anywhere in town on Lopez and turns 360 degrees, one will count several rabbits. When such a boom occurs in synchronicity with Island Marble restoration, host plant propagation is clearly restricted. So, one's perception of the rabbit populations is relative to time spent

---

[3] Issues of conflict and control inherent to this topic are discussed in Chapter Four, while conflicting information is discussed prominently in Chapter Three.

on the San Juan Islands. Moreover, for those who recognize this biophysical problem, solutions are quite readily identified and discussed. There must be fewer rabbits. However, when it comes to the sociocultural components (i.e., local concern for rabbit well-being), the problem's solution is rendered indiscernible. Thus, one finds in the *rabbit boom/bust cycle* problem of time another example of ontological quality predicting solvability and likelihood the issue is receiving practical consideration by conservation actors.

Another primarily biophysical problem of synchronization in this case is the potential for climate change to cause or exacerbate *caterpillar-host plant desynchronization.* Despite surviving the 20th century in apparently very low numbers, IMBs can be finicky creatures in some respects. In their first instar stage, having just hatched from an egg, IMB caterpillars feed only on a particular part of their host plant. As they progress through instar stages, they rely on different parts of the host plant. Thus, the plants must grow and bloom at just the right time that the caterpillars are hatching and feeding. Mike, a former FWS employee who had worked closely with the IMB, described the problem:

> If you have this tiny mismatch—because Island Marble can only feed on the newest buds. Its mouth parts of the caterpillar are so soft when it first emerges from its egg, it can only feed off of the newest part of the bud of the mustard plant. And so if that's—if you have this mismatch in timing, and that plant is too old, essentially the caterpillar starves because it can't eat.

This particular problem of synchronization is most apparent to those who work closely with the butterfly and its host plants. It is severe, and it is made formal as a concern in listing documents. Stakeholders expressed thoughtfulness about the likelihood of implementing solutions to this biophysical problem. Some offered that with care, the caterpillars and plants could be captively reared in synchronicity. Outside of captivity, however, and in the context of global climate change, the broad biophysical process of weather and ecology are, in their relative insolvability, causes for alarm.

Lastly, some stakeholders described a problem of *ignorance of butterfly lifecycles.* IMB lifecycles are of course quite different from those of humans. As described in Chapter One, they are annual creatures who spend much of their lives as eggs, caterpillars, chrysalises, and a short time in the sun as butterflies. Yet, here and elsewhere they are called and known by their butterfly form, obscuring the greater truth of their existence as things that crawl and things that lie still in transformation. One conservationist involved in the early years of IMB conservation, Larry, blamed public ignorance of butterfly lifecycles for its demise from Lopez Island and general contraction to American Camp. Larry told me:

> The part that people have so much trouble with is this is a resident butterfly, you know? People know about monarchs and they think that when they don't see butterflies they're gone. But the Island Marble is on San Juan 365 days of the year. And on every day of the year there's something that you can do that would kill it. You know? If it's—if you cut down that mustard plant while the caterpillar is feeding on it, it's gonna starve to death. If you burn the prairie while there's a pupa on the ground or if you till the soil while there's a pupa on the ground, you know, that's it. So people don't understand that the butterfly is still there when you can't see it. And that's what makes it so hard.

To those who are scholars of butterflies, their biophysical realities are readily apparent, and so then is the sociocultural ignorance that surrounds these realities. This location of the problem as dually sociocultural and biophysical results in more common observation of a solution. The San Juan Island community must become aware that the butterfly is not gone when it is not in flight. Individuals from FWS, WDFW, local NGOs, and NPS alike described current and future initiatives to solve the problem. Having identified a socio-biophysical problem and its subsequent solution, many collaborators work purposefully to prevent this severe problem of time from damning the butterfly's recovery a second time.

Applying Frameworks of Temporal Problems in Conservation Sociology

This chapter on the socio-biophysical nature of problems of time in IMB conservation is meant to accomplish a few things. First, it is intended to develop an applicable framework with which to identify and characterize the social components of problems of time in species conservation. As the chapter argues, such problems contain both sociocultural and biophysical realities, amounting to a socio-biophysical existence. Accounting for both realities results in a more complete understanding of the issues, their causes, and their solutions. Such social components are not always ignored by the scholars of the biophysical who dominate conservation work, but they are rarely systematically treated. Second, the study attempts to describe and explain one component process by which sociocultural inertia persists with regard to conservation issues. In other words, the chapter draws attention to issues of time not only because of their emergence as a theme in the interview data, but because of the apparent significance of these issues in understanding societal inaction on urgent and threatening environmental issues. Third, this chapter seeks to speak to and between the literatures of the sociology of time and environmental sociology, toward furthering discussions of environmental time. I here relate the work presented to these goals in turn before offering suggestions for future research in this vein, as well as a few concluding remarks.

First, by explicitly applying a critical realist ontology to issues of time in IMB conservation, I have attempted to develop a design which may be applied across time, place, and species to identify, describe, relate to the biophysical, and to develop solutions to the sociocultural components of species conservation having to do with the core aspect of time. I have attempted to explore the case of the IMB, present observed problems of time, describe their characteristics based on the framework's criteria, and to discuss potential solutions. In doing so, the data presented a rough pattern by which biophysical problems of time (or problems' biophysical components) appeared to receive greater practical treatment and solution-building by IMB stakeholders as pertinent objects of conservation action. It is important to clarify that all sociocultural problems of time discussed were raised by stakeholders and that these problems are readily identified and described by conservationists. However, where problems of time with more significant biophysical realities receive subsequent attention as conservation goals, research here suggests that sociocultural problems of time tend to remain the objects of only abstract discussion. Consider, for example, IMB stakeholders' willingness to entertain co-rearing IMBs and host plants, while their common oral history cites struggles to synchronize information across actors.

Additionally, the data presented a pattern that suggested in a broad sense that social positions dictate individuals' capacities to perceive the sociocultural or biophysical components of problems, and therefore their capacities to develop such solutions. This analysis cannot develop a systematic theory for how and why social positions dictate these perspectives, but it cannot ignore that this relativity of perception is an apparent phenomenon and one which has analogs in the physics and psychology of perception. For a tangible example, readers may consider that significant literacy and training are prerequisites to identifying and developing solutions to the ecological and biological matters of conservation (called here the "biophysical"). This chapter is suggesting, in plain terms, that social scientific literacy or similar training, such as political or educational experience, can operate as a prerequisite to identifying and developing solutions to sociocultural matters. Understanding this process is vital to species conservation, and as I here present this work as an example of conservation sociology, I recognize a necessity to legitimize sociocultural things as real, and in particular, to characterize the socio-biophysical problems of time not in the purely abstract or unscientific, but in the empirical, practical, and actionable realm of species conservation. The first step must be formalizing recognition that the sociocultural is equally as important, identifiable, and scientifically describable as the biophysical. The second step will be an interdisciplinary analysis of the full scope of socio-biophysical phenomena pertinent to conservation goals.

By way of example, identified problems of time in IMB conservation may be linked in a preliminary fashion to supplies of existing literature that may help inform contemporary IMB conservation work. To the issues of *residential turnover* and *increasing tourism*, there exists a growing body of literature in the environmental and rural sociologies that documents the multi-faceted social transformations experienced by communities undergoing concurrent rapid growth in the ecotourism sector and rising property values (Belsky 1999; Hunter et al. 2005; Jones 2005; Sherman 2018, 2021). The issue of *staff turnover* has little treatment in the conservation context but has been studied by social scientists researching other kinds of organizations such as hospitals (Hinshaw and Atwood 1984; Banaszak-Holl and Hines 1996; Donoghue and Castle 2009), substance abuse treatment centers (Knight et al. 2012), the tourism industry (Chalkiti and Sigala 2010), and more. *Seasonal employment* has been related to gender (Purcell 2000; Reid 2002; Vosko et al. 2003), welfare use (Brady et al. 2002), and social inequality (Fuller and Vosko 2008). The *pace of bureaucracy* is a very well-studied subject in sociology, analyses of bureaucratic structures being extant in foundational and contemporary sociological theory and research (Gouldner 1954; Pinchot and Pinchot 1994; Meier and Hill 2005). Social scientists of science itself have researched the *interrelatedness of funding and research* (Lave et al. 2010). There is already enough social scientific research in publication to synthesize knowledge regarding these issues and produce scientifically informed descriptions of and solutions to these problems as they relate to IMB conservation work. This then provides an example of the usefulness of conservation sociology.

Secondly, this chapter contributes to conversations regarding social inertia toward species conservation and environmental problems writ large, because it describes one way in which the sociological components of environmental problems systematically elude perception even among stakeholders who may be scientists or experts. Carolan (2005), as well as sociologists of time, offer a critique of the illusion (and subsequent superstition) of human exemptionalism. In its temporal form, this exemptionalism is characterized by a lack of reflexivity about sociocultural time, a belief that humans are set somehow outside of biophysical time, and a failure to recognize that at moments of human perception, all matters of time become jointly socio-biophysical. Thus, we must paradoxically dissect this socio-biophysical temporal reality into three ontological components in order to reveal the greater truth that they are all a unified whole. When we endeavor to make visible the sociocultural components of that which is usually perceived as biophysical or vice versa, we render more whole socio-biophysical realities that can then be addressed. When describing physical force, one must account for the material realities of the situation, i.e., mass. In the sociocultural context, one must describe the sociocultural analogs: resources, political will, cultural support, etc. Then, to fully calculate, one multiplies mass (or the sociocultural analog) by acceleration, thus accounting in some sense for time. So, in a conservation sociology, we must account not only for material reality on a socio-biophysical level, but also the rate at which this socio-biophysical reality is moving and changing.

Lastly, this chapter builds toward reconciling literature in environmental sociology and the sociology of time by offering one applied, case-based analysis of the issue of socioenvironmental time. Much further work is necessary in terms of research, theory-building, increased interdisciplinary work, and increased communication between European and North American sociologists. More particularly, this chapter is meant to lay a foundation for conversation about time to take place in the context of conservation sociology. Further qualitative research will help to identify which of these problems of time are particular to IMB conservation and which are more commonly found elsewhere. Quantitative studies might attempt to account for the ways in which organizational structure predicts response time to stimuli in conservation efforts, especially to answer the question of whether more or less centralized social structures respond more quickly. Additionally, quantitative research might develop alternate empirical approaches to more systematically identify and describe general characteristics of the kinds of problems of time identified here. Furthermore, quantitative work could attempt to test the burgeoning theory of the inherent tensions between dominant *linear* conceptions of sociocultural time and *cyclical* conceptions of biophysical time. In the contexts of accelerating climate change, rapid species extinction, and week-long butterfly flight times, these conversations may seem formal, esoteric, philosophical, and detached. However, if we do not begin somehow, sometime the task of implementing, with urgency and purpose, the sociological components of these problems of time into actionable conservation work, we may run out of time to solve them.

Chapter 6

Conclusion

This book has sought to do several things, from the meta-scientific description and positioning of conservation sociology, to weighing in on environmental sociology's discussions of sociopolitical inertia toward urgent environmental problems such as biodiversity loss, to formally recording a sort of history of the Island Marble Butterfly's (IMBs) conservation, to trying to develop knowledge that may be of use to IMB conservationists. Throughout, the book has put forth a series of articulations of what exactly the contribution of sociology may be to conservation science. This chapter revisits each substantive chapter's conclusions in turn before synthesizing them toward more comprehensive conclusions. This synthesis is organized into two parts, first considering case-specific conclusions regarding IMB conservation, then considering broad conclusions related to conservation and society. This discussion is followed by treatments of the generalizability and limitations of this study, as well as imperatives for future research. Lastly, the chapter concludes with some final thoughts on the IMB's past, present, and future, as well as that of species conservation writ large. This chapter is intended for sociological and non-sociological audiences alike and should provide a good resource for conservation actors to identify key takeaways of this research.

Chapter Three poses research questions related to the disparate norms, values, and beliefs IMB stakeholders hold with regard to the butterfly and its conservation, such as: How are conceptions of the IMB, its circumstances, and its conservation characterized among its stakeholders? How do disparate characterizations of these elements shape the collective conservation effort? The study finds that IMB stakeholders can be organized into three ideal-type groups based on the norms, values, and beliefs they adhere to with regard to IMB conservation: those *Skeptics*, who maintain that empirical research precedes best conservation practice; those *Collaborators*, who maintain that relationships facilitate best conservation practice; and those *Protectors*, who maintain that attention to the IMB's well-being precedes best conservation practice. The analysis applies Boundary Theories of the social production of scientific knowledge (Gieryn 1983; Star and Griesemer 1989) to further conclude that control of knowledge and meanings surrounding the IMB are not distributed evenly among these three stakeholder groups. Rather, control is currently held by the *Protectors*, *Protector* control is facilitated by the *Collaborators*, and *Skeptics* are currently operating at the margins of the production of IMB science. The broader conclusion of this chapter is that meaning and knowledge in conservation science and practice is not created in a vacuum, but rather results from contests and collaborations across groups holding different ideas. This finding implies the need for careful analysis of the social contexts from which conservation science and action are produced.

Chapter Four investigates the role of social power in the IMB's conservation effort, posing research questions such as: In what forms does power manifest in a conservation effort? How do IMB stakeholders perceive power as operating in conservation work, and is that perception congruent with power's actual function? How do conservation actors conceive of the relationship between the political-economic context in which their work takes place and the goals and obstacles of their particular conservation effort? Why was the IMB in particular set to be listed as an endangered species while so many other species are threatened, and the Trump administration was notoriously disengaged with conservation efforts? The chapter employs several sociological theories of power to organize its discussion, including Lukes' "Dimensions of Power" (Lukes 1986), Weber's "Authority" (Spencer 1970), and Gramsci's "Hegemony" (Bates 1975). The analysis concludes that there are salient distinctions between the realities of and IMB stakeholder's perceptions of decision-making power and ideological power in IMB conservation work. IMB stakeholders tend to describe decision-making as being collective while it is often individual, and they also tend to neglect to describe the function of ideological power or the relevance of a political-economic context to their work. Further, the study concludes that a capitalist political-economic context predicated on an ideological foundation of limitless growth is not only relevant to the IMB's particular case, but an essential social factor. This finding is supportive of a growing thesis in the social studies of conservation, which suggests that the systematic neoliberalization of species conservation efforts serves to contain the capacity of conservation work to identify and address problematic components of relevant political and economic systems (Büscher et al. 2012; Büscher et al. 2014). Thus, the IMB's prominent and successful conservation effort is concluded to be effective in part because it does not pose a threat to these dominant systems, and in fact, the IMB's conservation may be useful to them.

Chapter Five draws on the sociology of time and Carolan's Bhaskarian critical realist ontology of environmental sociology to describe temporally related obstacles to IMB conservation, both social and biophysical, and to prescribe solutions to these problems (2005). The chapter asks research questions such as: What are the natures of sociocultural and biophysical reckonings of time, and how do they relate to one another? In what ways does time generate dysfunction in a conservation effort? How do IMB stakeholders perceive different conservation problems related to time, and how is this perception related to the ontological assumptions that undergird the natural and social sciences? The chapter concludes that individuals' social positions result in variable perceptions of "problems of time" in IMB conservation. Moreover, IMB stakeholders tend to describe and identify sociocultural problems of time, but only to render prescriptions for conservation action when the problems are more biophysical in nature than sociocultural. This conclusion is asserted to have generalizable use when considering species conservation writ large, as this essential ontological distinction—the perception of social things as having their own *sui generis* existence, as empirically observable and describable as natural phenomena—is at the foundation of defining conservation sociology and its applied use. Indeed, Chapter Five exists here as a sort of template, as conservation efforts beyond the IMB's may be mapped out similarly into sociocultural, socio-biophysical, and biophysical problems, and their solutions described and implemented accordingly, thus more holistically addressing all factors relevant to a species' or ecosystem's well-being.

Conclusions for IMB Conservation

IMB conservation expresses many remarkable qualities: its rediscovery, its very low population count, its restriction to a non-native viable host plant, the heroic actions of a few individuals to keep the species from extinction, its location within a historic park on one small part of a unique island chain, and the fascinating debates within its conservation history. However, perhaps the most remarkable quality, and therefore most demanding of consideration here, is the fact that among the enormous number of insect species thought to be threatened worldwide, the IMB not only receives meaningful conservation support, but joined an exclusive group of only 48 insect species in the U.S. that are recognized as federally endangered. Moreover, this occurred in the context of a presidential administration notorious for its aversion to conservation practice. It is worth returning to and expanding upon the question: Why is the IMB, among all threatened species, listed under the ESA? Indeed, if we collectively consider the IMB's conservation effort to be the story of successful movements toward preventing the species from extinction, then better understanding its case should also help us to better understand sociopolitical inertia toward preventing the extinction of other species.

The overarching IMB-specific conclusion of this research is also a response to this question: the internal and contextual social qualities exhibited by IMB conservation facilitate its intensive protection under a general conservation regime characterized by neoliberalism (Igoe and Brockington 2007; Büscher et al. 2012). These qualities include: the environmentalist ethic, resident affluence, and ecotourist economy of the San Juan Islands; the location of the IMB within an already protected natural space at American Camp; the presence of a high number of large, suitable private properties on which small plots may be easily dedicated to host plant growth; the high social status of many of those most invested in IMB conservation science and work; the capacity for the butterfly to operate, like the southern resident killer whales, as a local attraction, natural commodity, or source of community pride; and the general absence of ways in which protecting the IMB, now that it has been exiled to its singular prairie, meaningfully obstructs any designs of a free market economy. This assertion is made here in full recognition that conservation science is generally intended (and by stakeholders here largely described) as being a matter of science foremost, and that interpreting the intervening social variables as holding extra-scientific sway contradicts this popular belief. This is a work of qualitative research, which cannot comment on the relative explanatory power of such variables. However, it is recommended based on this conclusion that future research investigate whether social variables do hold greater explanatory power in predicting species' listing than biological or ecological variables (e.g., rate of decline, taxa, population size, etc.).

Relative to most of the interview participants in this study, I spent only a small amount of time investigating the IMB. This work does not presume to produce answers to all of its various conservation obstacles, nor to challenge the species' conservation leadership on their past and present plans and actions. In particular, readers will have noted by this point that this study does not include a prominent accounting of the crucial biological and ecological aspects of the IMB's case, nor does the manuscript weigh on the essential question of whether the IMB warrants allocation of finite conservation resources. As outlined in Chapter Two, the conservation sociologist's role is to empirically describe social phenomena, to use sociological research and theory to illuminate these phenomena, and to participate in developing solutions to the phenomena that are obstructive to necessary and urgent conservation actions. In description, this study found salient discrepancies in stakeholders' perceptions of best conservation practices and of the IMB itself, in power held by individuals and groups in the conservation effort, and in perceptions of the nature of obstacles faced by the species. The study has used social theory to interpret the boundaries that exist within this scientific advocacy network, to interpret the role of power and ideology, to draw ontological distinctions between conservation sociology and conservation biology more generally, and to analyze the (dys)function of social time as an obstacle to IMB conservation. Collectively, these various findings suggest that social factors could be treated with more deliberate action and research in the IMB's case than they are at present. Doing so, however, requires careful reflection on both the concealed social factors that undergird the breadth and success of the IMB's conservation support, as well as those that undergird the firm limitations to that support.

Conclusions for General Species Conservation

In most social contexts, there is a code for what can and cannot be said. For example, it is generally customary in contemporary American society to avoid discussion of politics and religion while sharing dinner. There are comparable yet different codes to follow when one is in the workplace, on a date, on public transit, watching over children, or writing a book. The same is true of species conservation work; there are things that are permissible and things that are not. Components of this code factor in the previous chapters. The featured conflicts over truth and meaning in Chapter Three are sensitive topics to some stakeholders and matters of secrecy to others. Chapter Four points out both stakeholders' popular denial of individual decision-making and their systematic exclusion of political economy from conservation discussion. Chapter Five draws attention to the general exclusion of social phenomena from problem identification and solution-building in IMB conservation work. And, in sum, the manuscript's suggestion that more research take place as conservation sociology spotlights the marginalization of social scientific perspectives in extant conservation research. That in the context of butterfly conservation it is more permissible to discuss instars, mustards, and wasps than to discuss deregulation, austerity, or social class is an observation that lies at the heart of this work. However, these are the extant social conditions conservation work faces, as real as computers, cars, and penicillin, not a matter of political or ideological dispute, but of attention or neglect.

Of course, there are social factors that are permissible in the conservation context. Stakeholders will eagerly draw attention to a supportive or contentious local public, an expert/lay divide in knowledge, the necessity for strong interpersonal working relationships among stakeholders and organizations, and the specter of those government representatives in D.C.—some allies, some enemies. Despite its marginalization as a topic, a popular narrative of the function of the social does pervade species conservationism. As has been repeated, it is a growing contention among social scholars of conservation that this narrative follows the general logic of neoliberalism (Büscher et al. 2012). In this model, even as contemporary American conservation work pursues a stated goal at odds with the manifest impact of free market capitalism on extant ecology, conservation work also implicitly and explicitly relies on austerity, deregulation, and other political strategies for maintaining the supremacy of that economic system. For neoliberal conservation, is not that the American federal government is highly representative of the interests of multinational corporations and billionaires that it threatens species' well-being, but that it expresses the wrong composition of office-holding Democrats and Republicans. It is not that the lay public cannot play a role in species protection, but that they must accept a role designated by a professional/managerial class of career conservationists. It is not that interpersonal conflict in conservation collaboration belies its internal power dynamics, but that there are "too many cooks," and control is better off consolidated. Perhaps, then, social perspectives are generally marginalized from conservationism because they have the capacity to identify and critique its narrative of the social.

This conclusion is no indictment of individuals involved in IMB conservation work or in the preservation of any other species, ecosystem, or natural resource. As has been described several times in this manuscript, it is rather significant that the sociological perspective perceives social things as having existences and natures of their own. Thus, while the research presented here relies on the accounts of conservation actors and ethnographic data collected in and around such actions, its conclusions regard, as has been its stated goal, the social components of conservation. Moreover, it is not possible here to assert positively whether or not this conclusion identifies a "problem" of any kind with species conservation in its current form. Perhaps in the IMB's and other species' cases, this judgment may be determined by the ultimate capacity of a conservation effort to achieve its stated goals. Yet, in a context of rapid and widespread species extinction, and with an eye toward understanding how sociopolitical inertia toward solving this urgent environmental problem continues to persist, the present work does offer one over-arching and conclusory deliberation on the state of conservation: the admission of more explicitly sociological research may have the capacity to decouple conservation work from a neoliberal ideological paradigm toward one that features an understanding of the social that is rooted in the same empiricism that now guides conservationism's understanding of the natural.

Looking Forward

Generalizability

To what extent can the findings presented in this manuscript be generalized to other threatened species' conservation efforts? It is not possible to know until further research is conducted, but we can construct an educated guess by synthesizing existing research from environmental sociology, conservation biology, and related fields. This section discusses the ways in which the IMB's case is and is not translatable to other contexts. It argues that much of the context of IMB conservation is unlikely to be generalizable, yet the sociological phenomena detailed here are likely more generalizable to other conservation efforts than not.

The IMB's conservation context contains remarkable peculiarities. Its re-discovery, affinity for non-native host plants, isolation to a small National Historical Park, and location among the very particular community of San Juan Island render a set of contextual criteria unlikely to be identically paralleled. It is also a case of biophysical and sociological extremes: one of the most at-risk butterfly species in North America, existing in a community characterized by hyperbolic dichotomies of longevity and change, of from-the-land livelihoods and transitory recreation in a virtual ecotopia, of strong conservation ethic wrestling with strong currents of property exchange and development. It is a species capable of falling to extinction or rebounding explosively in a single season. It is symbolically liminal, a quintessential example of the rare charismatic microfauna, treasured invaluably by some San Juan Island residents and entirely unknown to others, at once beautiful, bright, full of personality, and yet to laymen nearly indistinguishable from other *Euchloe* or even the Cabbage White. However, in spite of all of that complexity, in relative terms IMB conservation is also remarkably simple. It is the domain of one state, one community, cooperating agencies and helpful non-profits in the absence of antagonistic forces. Perhaps most importantly, IMB conservation faces no real opposition and threatens no real private enterprise.

So, while the IMB appears, at least to a social scientist, practically unique in its biophysical conditions, its social conditions are special in some regards and common in others. In some ways the culture and social structure of San Juan Island are different even from nearby Lopez and Orcas Islands. Yet, the transformation of its rural, ecologically valuable context to one of increased attention from home-seekers and tourists especially from those in nearby Seattle is a transformation felt across the Pacific Northwest. The inter-organizational collaboration around IMB conservation that includes local and national NGOs, FWS, WDFW, NPS, universities and local governments is one that is mirrored now in the cases of nearly all threatened species in North America. The national and global economic and political contexts which trickle down impacts onto the IMB's case are felt by species elsewhere. The culture of the San Juan Islands is particular, but in an increasingly technologically connected world, even the islands are somewhat assimilated into a more broadly shared culture. And, the friendships, the mentorships, the collaborations, and employee-employer relationships occurring on a micro-sociological level in the IMB's case are likely to be mirrored elsewhere. Thus, readers should take care in applying findings here to other contexts, but one should also acknowledge that much of what is true of the sociology of the IMB's conservation will be true of the sociology of other butterfly, insect, and animal species beyond.

Practical Applications

One goal of this project has been to synthesize perspectives among stakeholders in order to find and present practical solutions to challenges facing the IMB. Readers with conservation backgrounds or readers close to the IMB conservation effort may be able to infer such solutions from some of the work presented here, and each substantive chapter has attempted to briefly comment on potential implications of the research. However, it is worth reviewing the key practical contributions of the work. As the manuscript has suggested many times, these practical suggestions may seem unusual given the overwhelmingly biological and ecological emphasis of typical conservation practices. However, this review of key practical contributions will of course continue to emphasize the social components and will only reflect what has been found in the research presented in Chapters Three through Five.

IMB stakeholders attested to the need for a strong collaborative group. Chapter Three considers that such a desired group may exhibit different characteristics depending on who one asks. However, the notion that collaboration is an integral part of the development of knowledge and practice in IMB conservation is well supported by this research. I recommend that IMB stakeholders maintain strong collaboration even through conflict, recognizing that conflict and the challenging of ideas is a necessary part of the production of science and practice, and that it is particularly through confronting differences that advancement will result. Stakeholders generally called for increased communication and transparency, and I find support for both of these calls. Chapter Four finds that stakeholders should increase their reflexivity with regard to the operation of hegemony and dominant capitalist ideology in their conservation work. Existential forces such as climate change, economic markets, and political-economic frameworks that guide understandings should be brought to the forefront of conversation. IMB conservationists should discuss openly the potential impacts of local and global issues that may affect IMB livelihood, be they ecological or social, without the interference of legitimating rationales that insist that the status quo is by definition natural, good, right, and/or immutable. Furthermore, stakeholders identified a number of social components of IMB conservation, particularly related to social timekeeping and the variation between natural and social timekeeping systems. Further research is necessary to explicate many of these individual factors, but research suggests generally that stakeholders can and should systematically identify such social factors and consider subsequent solutions, as they would treat similar ecological problems. These practical suggestions share a common thread: increased application of sociological research to the conservation program will result in increased capability of the collaboration to identify, describe, discuss, and solve the socioenvironmental problems related to IMB conservation, which are as real and describable as the ecological problems.

Key Takeaways

For the purpose of maximum clarity, the key conclusions that I draw from this research project are as follows:

1. Consensuses exist in IMB conservation. Consensuses are derived from a process of conflict. Consensuses are in and of themselves a product of and producer of power dynamics within the conservation effort.

2. Consensus accounts exclude political economy from IMB conservation discussion and subsequently from being addressed by IMB conservation action. This exclusion is reproduced because conservation work takes place in civil society, and a fundamental function of civil society is to legitimate extant political-economic structures.

3. As such, IMB conservation work is fundamentally a project that, rather than seeking to disrupt capitalist social processes that cause the extinction of species, seeks to insulate specifically the IMB from extinction without disrupting those processes and, if possible, to take place in mutual benefit with those processes.

4. Moreover, as identification of social phenomena related to species conservation tends toward implication of these capitalist social processes as both causes of extinction and obstacles to conservation, social science itself is thus systematically excluded from conservation work. While social problems are identified, many are not considered to be within the purview of IMB conservation work or are considered natural and/or inevitable.

5. Consequently, sociopolitical inertia toward abating species extinction appears to be reproduced out of a complex process of systematic avoidance of applying sociological perspectives to conservation work and a continued privileging of natural scientific perspectives that do not implicate the underlying social processes that result in extinction. This implies that species such as the IMB are more likely to be the subjects of successful conservation efforts if those efforts participate in reproducing extant capitalist processes rather than disrupting them.

6.   Thus, one part of the solution to sociopolitical inertia toward abating species extinction might be the increased production of conservation sociology, which, as I have attempted to provide example of through this study of the IMB, can provide description, theorization, and prescriptions for application to a conservation effort.

Final Reflections & Conclusions

This book has been motivated by an idea that is perhaps best articulated by influential American environmental lawyer Gus Speth in a 2015 interview about his memoir, *Angels by the River*:

> I used to think that the top environmental problems were biodiversity loss, ecosystem collapse and climate change. I thought that thirty years of good science could address these problems. I was wrong. The top environmental problems are selfishness, greed, and apathy, and to deal with these we need a cultural and spiritual transformation. And we scientists don't know how to do that.

I agree with Speth that the natural sciences cannot alone prevent an ecological calamity such as the current rate of biodiversity loss on Earth. I disagree that selfishness, greed, and apathy are the top environmental problems or the core human causes of biodiversity loss, and I disagree that a cultural and spiritual transformation is most needed. Rather, the usefulness of a sociological perspective on biodiversity loss is that it renders visible the concealed truth that *social structures* and the organization of human society in its current form are the underlying causes of most environmental problems. These causes are not invested in the hearts and minds of individuals, but manifest rather in the things we create between us, the enduring and pervasive apparatuses of the social: our institutions, our corporations, our markets, our shared ideas, and our inventions. What is needed is not an abstract plea for human spirituality to become transformed. We carry internally already the spirit of a conservation ethic. Our machines, however, have no spirits to transform—only programming. What is needed is that the social structural culprits of this calamity, whether cultural, economic, political, or philosophical, be illuminated. They must be identified, named, investigated, described, understood, and rehabilitated—reprogrammed. I am writing of course of the present global political-economic apparatus of endless growth capitalism, which is ultimately responsible for contemporary environmental problems from anthropogenic climate change to the near extinction of the Island Marble Butterfly. When environmental stakeholders—even those who would privately implicate political economy in their diagnoses—systematically expel discussion of this root cause from our conversation, science, and solution-making, we reify it as natural and immutable. Rather, this system is designed, is transformable, and must urgently be transformed. Let this research project be a small and humble step toward a human world that does not annihilate, in utter negligence and with no recourse for redemption, something so precious as the good, green gold of spring.

Appendix A

Sample Interview Guide

❖ Professional Experience with Island Marble

  o Would you briefly describe your experience working with the Island Marble Butterfly?

  o What motivated you to work w/ Island Marble?

  o If still working: How do you believe initiative is progressing?

  o If not working: How did you come to stop?

  o Perception of the conservation effort overall?

  o Assessment of own contribution?

❖ Interdisciplinary Collaboration

  o To what extent did you feel that you were taking part in a collaboration with other experts?

  o Assess collaboration? Interested in barriers and moments of success.

    ▪ Problems? Benefits?

  o Specifically, rifts between disciplines/professions? Professions that communicated well?

  o Bureaucratic or governmental obstacles? Personal obstacles? Scientific obstacles? What seemed to cause the greatest barrier?

  o Experience with other key individuals?

❖ Obstacles to Conservation Goals

  o What do you perceive as the primary obstacles to protecting the Island Marble Butterfly?

  o How do you believe these obstacles will be overcome?

  o What needs to occur for the Island Marble to avoid extinction, ecologically or socially?

❖ Personal Information

  o Professional Title?

  o Educational attainment?

  o Kind of degree?

- o   Similar experiences working with other species?
- o   Age?
- o   Political affiliation?
- o   Where originally from?

References

Abson, D. J., H. von Wehrden, S. Baumgärtner, J. Fischer, J. Hanspach, W. Härdtle, H. Heinrichs, A. M. Klein, D. J. Lang, P. Martens, and D. Walmsley. 2014. "Ecosystem Services as Boundary Object for Sustainability." *Ecological Economics* 103:29-37.

Adam, Barbara. 2002. "The Gendered Time Politics of Globalization: Of Shadowlands and Elusive Justice." *Feminist Review* 70:3-29.

Affolderbach, Julia, Alex Clapp, and Roger Hayter. 2012. "Environmental Bargaining and Boundary Organizations: Remapping British Columbia's Great Bear Rainforest." *Annals of the Association of American Geographers* 102(6):1391-1408.

Agrawal, Arun, and Clark C. Gibson. 2001. *Communities and the Environment: Ethnicity, Gender, and the State in Community-Based Conservation.* Piscataway, NJ: Rutgers University Press.

Agarwal, Bina. 2009. "Gender and Forest Conservation: The Impact of Women's Participation in Community Forest Governance." *Ecological Economics* 68:2785-2799.

Agnone, Jon. 2007. "Amplifying Public Opinion: The Policy Impact of the U.S. Environmental Movement." *Social Forces* 85(4):1593-1620.

Aguiar, Luis L. M., and Christopher J. Schneider. 2012. *Researching Amongst Elites: Challenges and Opportunities in Studying Up.* New York, NY: Routledge.

Allen, Barbara L. 2004. "Shifting Boundary Work: Issues and Tensions in Environmental Health Science in the Case of Grand Bois, Louisiana." *Science as Culture* 13(4):429-448.

Aminzade, Ronald. 1992. "Historical Sociology and Time." *Sociological Methods & Research* 20(4):456-480.

Ando, Amy W. 1999. "Waiting to Be Protected under the Endangered Species Act: The Political Economy of Regulatory Delay." *The Journal of Law & Economics* 42(1):29-60.

Andrews, Tom. 2012. "What is Social Constructionism?" *The Grounded Theory Review* 11(1):39-46.

Arendt, Hannah. 1970. *On Violence.* Orlando, FL: Houghton Mifflin Harcourt Publishing Company.

Artelle, Kyle A., Melanie Zurba, Jonaki Bhattacharyya, Diana E. Chan, Kelly Brown, Jess Housty, and Faisal Moola. 2019. "Supporting Resurgent Indigenous-led Governance: A Nascent Mechanism for Just and Effective Conservation." *Biological Conservation* 240:108284.

Ban, Natalie C., Alejandro Frid, Mike Reid, Barry Edgar, Danielle Shaw, and Peter Siwallace. 2018. "Incorporate Indigenous Perspectives for Impactful Research and Effective Management." *Nature Ecology & Evolution* 2:1680-1683.

Banaszak-Holl, Jane, and Marilyn A. Hines. 1996. "Factors Associated with Nursing Home Staff Turnover." *The Gerontologist* 36(4):512-517.

Bates, Thomas R. 1975. "Gramsci and the Theory of Hegemony." *Journal of the History of Ideas* 36(2):351-366.

Bazeley, Patricia, and Lyn Richards. 2000. *The NVivo Qualitative Project Book.* Thousand Oaks, CA: Sage Publications Inc.

Beck, Ulrich. 1992. *Risk Society: Towards a New Modernity.* Newbury Park, CA: Sage Publications.

Becker, Penny Edgell. 2000. "Boundaries and Silences in a Post-Feminist Sociology." *Sociology of Religion* 61(4):399-408.

Bekoff, Marc. 2013. *Ignoring Nature No More: The Case for Compassionate Conservation.* Chicago, IL: University of Chicago Press.

Belsky, Jill M. 1999. "Misrepresenting Communities: The Politics of Community-Based Rural Ecotourism in Gales Point Manatee, Belize." *Rural Sociology* 64(4):641-666.

Belsky, Jill M. 2002. "Beyond the Natural Resource and Environmental Sociology Divide: Insights from a Transdisciplinary Perspective." *Society & Natural Resources* 15(3):269-280.

Bennett, Nathan J., Robin Roth, Sarah C. Klain, Kai Chan, Patrick Christie, Douglas A. Clark, Georgina Cullman, Deborah Curran, Trevor J. Durbin, Graham Epstein, Alison Greenberg, Michael P. Nelson, John Sandlos, Richard Stedman, Tara L. Teel, Rebecca Thomas, Diogo Veríssimo, and Carina Wyborn. 2017. "Conservation Social Science: Understanding and Integrating Human Dimensions to Improve Conservation." *Biological Conservation* 205:93-108.

Bergmann, Werner. 1992. "The Problem of Time in Sociology: An Overview of the Literature on the State of Theory and Research on the 'Sociology of Time', 1900-82. *Time Society* 1:81.

Berkes, Fikret. 2021. *Advanced Introduction to Community-based Conservation.* Northhampton, MA: Edward Elgar Publishing.

Bernstein, Richard J. 2011. "Hannah Arendt's Reflections on Violence and Power." *Iris* III:3-30.

Besek, Jordan F., and Richard York. 2019. "Toward a Sociology of Biodiversity Loss." *Social Currents* 6(3):239-254.

Bhaskar, R. 2005. *Critical Realism and the Theory and Practice of Interdisciplinarity.* Lecture presented at the 27th World Congress of the International Institute of Sociology, Stockholm Sweden.

Black, Scott Hoffman, and Mace Vaughan. 2002. "Petition to Emergency List the Island Marble Butterfly (*Euchloe ausonides insulanus*) as an Endangered Species under the U.S. Endangered Species Act." The Xerces Society, Center for Biological Diversity, Friends of the San Juans, and the Northwest Ecosystem Alliance.

Black, Scott Hoffman. 2012. "Invertebrates and the Endangered Species Act." *WINGS: Essays on Invertebrate Conservation* Spring:22-28.

Bourdieu, Pierre. 1963. "La Societe traditionnelle. Attitude a l'egard du temps et conduit economique." Pp. 24-44 in *Sociologie du Travail.*

Bourdieu, Pierre. 1968. "The Attitude of the Algerian Peasant Toward Time." Pp.55-72 in *Mediterranean Countrymen,* edited by J. Pitt-Rivers. Paris: The Hague.

Brady, Henry E., Mary Sprague, Fredric C. Gey and Michael Wiseman. 2002. "Seasonal Employment Dynamics and Welfare Use in Agricultural and Rural California Counties." Pp.147-175 in *Rural Dimensions of Welfare Reform*, edited by Bruce A. Wever, Greg J. Duncan, and Leslie A. Whitener. Kalamazoo, MI: W.E. Upjohn Institute for Employment Research.

Brand, Fridolin S., and Kurt Jax. 2007. "Focusing the Meaning(s) of Resilience: Resilience as a Descriptive Concept and a Boundary Object." *Ecology and Society* 12(1):23 [online] http://www.ecologyandsociety.org/vol12/iss1/art23/

Breitmeier, Helmut, Arild Underdal and Oran R. Young. 2011. "The Effectiveness of International Environmental Regimes: Comparing and Contrasting Findings from Quantitative Research." *International Studies Review* 13(4):579-605.

Brooke, Cassandra. 2008. "Conservation and Adaptation to Climate Change." *Conservation Biology* 22(6):1471-1476.

Brosius, J. Peter. 2006. "Common Ground between Anthropology and Conservation Biology." *Conservation Biology* 20(3):683-685.

Brown, Gardner M. and Jason F. Shogren. 1998. "Economics of the Endangered Species Act." *Journal of Economic Perspectives* 12(3):3-20.

Budowski, Gerardo. 1976. "Tourism and Environmental Conservation: Conflict, Coexistence, or Symbiosis?" *Environmental Conservation* 3(1):27-31.

Burawoy, Michael. 1998. "The Extended Case Method." *Sociological Theory* 16(1):143-144.

Burawoy, Michael. 2009. *The Extended Case Method: Four Countries, Four Decades, Four Great Transformations, and One Theoretical Tradition*. Berkley, CA: University of California Press.

Burger, Joanna. 2000. "Landscapes, Tourism, and Conservation." *The Science of the Total Environment* 249:39-49.

Burrows, Roger. 2016. "'Studying Up' in the Era of Big Data." In *An End to the Crisis of Empirical Sociology? Trends and Challenges in Social Research*, edited by Linda McKie and Louise Ryan. New York, NY: Routledge.

Büscher, Bram. 2010. "Anti-Politics as a Political Strategy: Neoliberalism and Transfrontier Conservation in South Africa." *Development and Change* 4(1):29-51.

Büscher, Bram, Sian Sullivan, Katja Neves, Jim Igoe, and Dan Brockington. 2012. "Towards a Synthesized Critique of Neoliberal Biodiversity Conservation." *Capitalism Nature Socialism* 2:4-30.

Büscher, Bram, Wolfram Dressler, and Robert Fletcher. 2014. *Nature Inc.: Environmental Conservation in the Neoliberal Age*. Tucson, AZ: The University of Arizona Press.

Büscher, Bram, and Robert Fletcher. 2020. *The Conservation Revolution: Radical Ideas for Saving Nature Beyond the Anthropocene*. Brooklyn, NY: Verso.

Buttel, Frederick H. 1978. "Environmental Sociology: A New Paradigm." *The American Sociologist* 13(4):252-256.

Buttel, Frederick H. 2003. "Environmental Sociology and the Explanation of Environmental Reform." *Organization & Environment* 16(3):306-344.

Buttigieg, Joseph A. 1995. "Gramsci on Civil Society." *boundary 2* 22(3):1-32.

Cahill, Rowan. 2007. "On Winning the 40 Hour Week." *Illawarra Unity* 7(1):16-25.

Caine, Ken J. 2016. "Blurring the Boundaries of Environmentalism: The Role of Canadian Parks and Wilderness Society as a Boundary Organization in Northern Conservation Planning." *Rural Sociology* 81(2):194-223.

Caldwell, Christopher. 2019. "The Problem with Greta Thunberg's Climate Activism." *The New York Times* August 2, 2019. https://www.nytimes.com/2019/08/02/opinion/climate-change-greta-thunberg.html Accessed February 2, 2020.

Camou-Guerrero, Andrés, Victoria Reyes-García, Miguel Martínez-Ramos, and Alejandro Casas. 2008. "Knowledge and Use Value of Plant Species in a Rarámuri Community: A Gender Perspective for Conservation." *Human Ecology* 36:259-272.

Campbell, Jock, and Philip Townsley. 2012. "Biodiversity and Poverty in Coastal Environments." Pp. 100-112 in *Biodiversity Conservation and Poverty Alleviation: Exploring the Evidence for a Link*, edited by D. Roe, J. Elliott, C. Sandbrook, and M. Walpole. Hoboken, NJ: John Wiley & Sons.

Cannon, John R. 1996. "Whooping Crane Recovery: A Case Study in Public and Private Cooperation in the Conservation of Endangered Species." *Conservation Biology* 10(3):813-821.

Cardinale, Bradley J., J. Emmett Duffy, Andrew Gonzalez, David U. Hooper, Charles Perrings, Patrick Venail, Anita Narwani, Georgina M. Mace, David Tilman, David A. Wardle, Ann P. Kinzig, Gretchen C. Daily, Michel Loreau, James B. Grace, Anne Larigauderie, Diane Srivastava, and Shahid Naeem. 2012. "Biodiversity loss and its impact on humanity." *Nature* 486(7401):59-67.

Carolan, Michael S. 2005. "Society, Biology, and Ecology: Bringing Nature Back Into Sociology's Disciplinary Narrative Through Critical Realism." *Organization & Environment* 18(4):393-421.

Carolan, Michael S. 2008. "From Patent Law to Regulation: The Ontological Gerrymandering of Biotechnology." *Environmental Politics* 17(5):749-765.

Carr, Anna, and Roger Wilkinson. 2005. "Beyond Participation: Boundary Organizations as a New Space for Farmers and Scientists to Interact." *Society & Natural Resources* 18(3):255-265.

Catton, William R., and Riley E. Dunlap. 1978. "Environmental Sociology: A New Paradigm." *The American Sociologist* 13:41-49.

Center for Biological Diversity. 2019. "The Endangered Species Act: A Wild Success." Retrieved October 1, 2019 https://www.biologicaldiversity.org/campaigns/esa_wild_success/index.html

Chalkiti, Kalotina, and Marianna Sigala. 2010. "Staff Turnover in the Greek Tourism Industry." *International Journal of Contemporary Hospitality Management* 22(3):335-359.

Chomsky, Noam, and Michel Foucault. 1971. "Human Nature: Justice vs. Power." Retrieved October 2, 2019 (https://chomsky.info/1971xxxx/).

Christensen, Ken. 2017. "On a Wing and a Prayer: A Butterfly Rescue on San Juan Island." *OPB* Oct. 26, 2017. https://www.opb.org/television/programs/ofg/segment/washington-island-marble-butterfly-san-juan-island/ Accessed February 4, 2020.

Cifrić, Ivan. 2010. "Ekologija veremena. Vrijeme kao integrativni I dezintegrativni čimbenik." *Socijalna ekologija* 19(1):5-32.

Cifrić, Ivan and Tijana Trako. 2010. "Društvo I okoliš u vermenskoj perspektivi. O sociologiji vremena I menadžmentu vremena." *Sociologija I prostor* 48(1):19049.

Clark, Brett, and Richard York. 2005. "Carbon Metabolism: Global Capitalism, Climate Change, and the Biosphere." *Theory and Society* 34:391-428.

Clark, Brett and John Bellamy Foster. 2009. "Ecological Imperialism and the Global Metabolic Rift: Unequal Exchange and the Guano/Nitrates Trade." *International Journal of Comparative Sociology* 50(3-4):311-334.

Clayton, Susan and Amara Brook. 2005. "Can Psychology Help Save the World? A Model for Conservation Psychology." *Analyses of Social Issues and Public Policy* 5(1):87-102

Cockburn, Jessica, Mathieu Rouget, Rob Slotow, Debra Roberts, Richard Boon, Errol Douwes, Sean O'Donoghue, Colleen Downs, Shomen Mukherjee and Walter Muskawa. 2016. "How to Build Science-Action Partnerships for Local Land-Use Planning and Management: Lessons from Durban, South Africa." *Ecology and Society* 21(1):28.

Cook, Carly N., Michael B. Mascia, Mark W. Schwartz, Hugh P. Possingham, and Richard A. Fuller. 2013. "Achieving Conservation Science that Bridges the Knowledge-Action Boundary." *Conservation Biology* 27(4):669-678.

Cordano, Mark, Stephanie Welcomer, Robert F. Scherer, Lorena Pradenas, and Víctor Parada. 2010. "Three Theories of Pro-Environmental Behavior: A Comparison Between Business Students of Chile and the United States." *Environment and Behavior* 43(5):634-657.

Czech, Brian, Paul R. Krausman, and Rena Borkhataria. 1998. "Social Construction, Political Power, and the Allocation of Benefits to Endangered Species." *Conservation Biology* 12(5):1103-1112.

Czech, Brian, and Paul R. Krausman. 2001. *The Endangered Species Act: History, Conservation Biology, and Public Policy.* Baltimore, MD: The Johns Hopkins University Press.

Damania, Richard, and Erwin H. Bulte. 2001. "The Economics of Captive Breeding and Endangered Species Conservation." *CIES Working Paper* No. 0139:1-44.

Damania, Richard, and Erwin H. Bulte. 2007. "The Economics of Wildlife Farming and Endangered Species Conservation." 62(3-4):461-472.

Danermark, Berth, Erkström, Jakobson, Liselotte, and Jan Ch. Karlsson. 2005. *Explaining Society: An Introduction to Critical Realism in the Social Sciences.* New York, NY: Routledge.

Devall, W. B. 1970. "Conservation: An Upper-middle Class Social Movement: A Replication." *Journal of Leisure Research* 2(2):123-126.

Donoghue, Christopher and Nicholas G. Castle. 2009. "Leadership Styles of Nursing Home Administrators and Their Association with Staff Turnover." *The Gerontologist* 49(2):166-174.

Dunlap, Riley E., George H. Gallup Jr., and Alec M. Gallup. 1993. "Of Global Concern: Results of the Health of the Planet Survey." *Environment: Science and Policy for Sustainable Development* 35(9):7-39.

Dunlap, Riley E. 1995. "Public Opinion and Environmental Policy" Pp. 63-114 in *Environmental Politics and Policy: Theories and Evidence*, edited by James P. Lester. Durham, NC: Duke University Press.

Dunlap, Riley E., Chenyang Xiao, and Aaron M. McCright. 2001. "Politics and Environment in America: Partisan and Ideological Cleavages in Public Support for Environmentalism." *Environmental Politics* 10(4):23-48.

Dunlap, Riley E. 2008. "The New Environmental Paradigm Scale: From Marginality to Worldwide Use." *The Journal of Environmental Education* 40(1):3-18.

Dunlap, Riley E., and Richard York. 2008. "The Globalization of Environmental Concern and the Limits of the Postmaterialist Values Explanation: Evidence from Four Multinational Surveys." *Sociological Quarterly* 49(3):529-563.

Durkheim, Émile. 1951. *Suicide: A Study in Sociology* (1st pub. 1897), edited by George Simpson. Translated by John A. Spaulding, and George Simpson. Glencoe, IL: Free Press.

Durkheim, Émile. 1982. *The Rules of Sociological Method and Selected Texts on Sociology and its Method*, edited by Steven Lukes. Translated by W. D. Halls New York, NY: Free Press.

Elder, Glen H. Jr., Monica Kirkpatrick Johnson, and Robert Crosnoe. 2003. "The Emergence and Development of Life Course Theory." Pp. 3-19 in *Handbook of the Life Course*, edited by Jeylan T. Mortimer, and Michael J. Shanahan. Boston, MA: Springer US.

Elliott, Joanna and Daudi Sumba. 2012. "Conservation Enterprise: What Works, Where and for Whom?" Pp. 206-222 in *Biodiversity Conservation and Poverty Alleviation: Exploring the Evidence for a Link*, edited by D. Roe, J. Elliott, C. Sandbrook and M. Walpole. Hoboken, NJ: John Wiley & Sons.

Esbjörn-Hargens, Sean. 2010. "An Ontology of Climate Change: Integral Pluralism and the Enactment of Multiple Objects." *Journal of Integral Theory and Practice* 5(1):143-174.

Flatt, Courtney. 2018. "A Butterfly Only Found in the Northwest is Headed for Endangered Species List." *NWPB/Earthfix*. April 11, 2018. https://www.opb.org/news/article/butterfly-endangered-san-juan-island-marble-list/ Accessed February 2, 2020.

Fleckenstein, John, and Ann Potter. 1999. "1997, 1998 project summary Puget prairie butterfly surveys." Washington Department of Natural Resources and Washington Department of Fish and Wildlife, Olympia, Washington.

Fletcher, Robert. 2012. "Using the Master's Tools? Neoliberal Conservation and the Evasion of Inequality." *Development and Change* 43(1):295-317.

Fletcher, Robert. 2014. "Orchestrating Consent: Post-Politics and Intensification of NatureTM Inc. at the 2012 World Conservation Congress." *Conservation and Society* 12(3):329-342.

Forester, Deborah J., and Gary E. Machlis. 1996. "Modeling Human Factors that Affect the Loss of Biodiversity." *Conservation Biology* 10(4):1253-1263.

Foster, John Bellamy. 1999. "Marx's Theory of Metabolic Rift: Classical Foundations for Environmental Sociology." *American Journal of Sociology* 105(2):366-405.

Foucault, Michel. 1980. *Power/Knowledge: Selected Interviews & Other Writings, 1972-1977*, edited by Colin Gordon. New York, NY: Pantheon Books.

Fox, Helen E., Caroline Christian, J. Cully Nordby, Oliver R. W. Pergrams, Garry D. Peterson, and Christopher R. Pyke. 2006. "Perceived Barriers to Integrating Social Science and Conservation."

Franks, Jeremy. 2010. "Boundary Organizations for Sustainable Land Management: The Example of Dutch Environmental Co-operatives." *Ecological Economics* 2(15):283-295.

Frickel, Scott M. 2004. *Chemical Consequences: Environmental Mutagens, Scientist Activism, and the Rise of Genetic Toxicology.* New Brunswick, NJ: Rutgers University Press.

Frickel, Scott, Sarah Gibbon, Jeff Howard, Joanna Kempner, Gwen Ottinger, and David J. Hess. 2010. "Undone Science: Charting Social Movement and Civil Society Challenges to Research Agenda Setting." *Science, Technology, & Human Values* 35(4): 444-473.

Fuller, Sylvia, and Leah F. Vosko. 2008. "Temporary Employment and Social Inequality in Canada: Exploring Intersections of Gender, Race and Immigration Status." *Social Indicators Research* 88(1):31-50.

Gaard, Greta. 2001. "Women, Water, Energy: An Ecofeminist Approach." *Organization & Environment* 14(2):157-172.

Gadgil, Madhav, Fikret Berkes, and Carl Folke. 1993. "Indigenous Knowledge for Biodiversity Conservation." *Ambio* 22:151-156.

Gamboa, Glenn. 2021. "Bezos Plans to Spend $10 Billion by 2030 on Climate Change." AP News 3/9/2021. Retrieved July 3, 2021. https://apnews.com/article/climate-climate-change-jeff-bezos-bee1aea9cffc377400048dcb5b7405f0

Gates, Bill. 2021. *How to Avoid Climate Disaster: The Solutions We Have and the Breakthroughs We Need.* New York, NY: Random House Inc.

Geißler, K.A. 1993. "Anfang und Ende. Zur Sozialökologie der Zeitordnung." Pp. 179-185 in *Ökologie der Zeit - Vom Finden der rechten Zeitmaße,* edited by M. Held, and K. A. Geißler. Stuggart: S. Hirzel Verlag

Gieryn, Thomas F. 1983. "Boundary-Work and the Demarcation of Science from Non-Science: Strains and Interests in Professional Ideologies of Scientists." *American Sociological Review* 48:781-795.

Gieryn, Thomas F. 1999. *Cultural Boundaries of Science: Credibility of the Line.* Chicago, IL: Aldine.

Glaser, Barney G., and Anselm L. Strauss. 1999. *Discovery of Grounded Theory: Strategies for Qualitative Research.* New York, NY: Routledge.

Gould, Kenneth A., David N. Pellow, and Allan Schnaiberg. 2008. *Treadmill of Production: Injustice and Unsustainability in the Global Economy.* Boulder, CO: Paradigm Publishers.

Gould, Stephen Jay. 1987. *Time's Arrow, Time's Cycle: Myth and Metaphor in the Discovery of Geological Time.* Cambridge, MA: Harvard University Press.

Gouldner, Alvin W. 1954. *Patterns of Industrial Bureaucracy.* New York, NY: Free Press.

Gray, Noella J. 2016. "The Role of Boundary Organizations in Co-Management: Examining the Politics of Knowledge Integrations in a Marine Protected Area in Belize." *International Journal of the Commons* 10(2):1013-1034.

Guppy, Crispin, and Jon Shepard. 2001. *Butterflies of British Columbia: Including Western Alberta, Southern Yukon, the Alaska Panhandle, Washington, Northern*

Oregon, Northern Idaho, and Northwestern Montana. Vancouver, B.C: University of British Columbia Press.

Gurvitch, Georges. 1964. *The Spectrum of Social Time*. Dordrecht, D: Reidel Pub. Co.

Gurvitch, Georges. 1973. "Social Structure and the Multiplicity of Times." Pp. 171-84 in *Sociological Theory*, edited by Edward A. Tiryakian. London, UK: Routledge.

Gustafsson, Karin M., Anurag A. Agrawal, Bruce V. Lewenstein, and Steven A. Wolf. 2015. "The Monarch Butterfly through Time and Space: The Social Construction of an Icon." *BioScience* 65(6):612-622.

Guston, David H. 2001. "Boundary Organizations in Environmental Policy and Science: An Introduction." *Science, Technology, & Human Values* 26(4):399-408.

Gramsci, Antonio. 1992-2007. *Prison Notebooks*. (Ed. by Joseph A. Buttigieg) New York, NY: Columbia University Press.

Haenn, Nora. 2016. "The Middle-Class Conservationist: Social Dramas, Blurred Identity Boundaries, and Their Environmental Consequences in Mexican Conservation." *Current Anthropology* 57(2):197-218.

Haines-Young, Roy and Marion Potschin. 2010."The Links Between Biodiversity, Ecosystem Services and Human Well-Being." Ch. 6 in *Ecosystem Ecology: A New Synthesis*, edited by D. Raffaelli, and C. Frid. New York, NY: Cambridge University Press.

Halpern, Megan K. 2011. "Across the Great Divide: Boundaries and Boundary Objects in Art and Science." *Public Understanding of Science* 21(8):922-937

Hanson, Thor, Ann Potter, James Miskelly, and Susan Vernon. 2009. "Surveys for the Island Marble Butterfly (*Euchloe ausonides insulanus*) in San Juan County, Washington, 2008." Washington Department of Fish and Wildlife, Olympia, WA.

Hanson, Thor, Ann Potter, and Susan Vernon. 2010. "Surveys for Island Marble Butterfly (*Euchloe ausonides insulanus*) in San Juan County, Washington, 2009." Washington Department of Fish and Wildlife, Olympia, WA.

Harrington, Winston, Richard D. Morgenstern, and Thomas Sterner. 2004. *Choosing Environmental Policy: Comparing Instruments and Outcomes in the United States and Europe*. Washington, DC: Resources for the Future.

Harvey, F., and N. Chrisman. 1998. "Boundary Objects and the Social Construction of GIS Technology." *Environment & Planning* 39(9):1683-1695.

Hassard, John. 1990. *The Sociology of Time*. New York, NY: St. Martin's Press.

Hassard, John, and Keith Grint. 1999. "Images of Time in Work and Organization." Pp.327-344 in *Studying Organization: Theory and Method*, edited by Stewart R. Clegg, and Cynthia Hardy. Newbury Park, CA: Sage Publications.

Hastings, Jesse G. 2011. "International Environmental NGOs and Conservation Science and Policy: A Case from Brazil." *Coastal Management* 39(3):317-335.

Held, M. 1993. "Zeitmaße für die Umwelt. Auf dem Weg zu einer Ökologie der Zeit."

Hinshaw, Ada Sue, and Jan R. Atwood. 1984. "Nursing Staff Turnover, Stress, and Satisfaction: Models, Measures, and Management." *Annual Review of Nursing Research* 1:133-153.

Hoban, Sean and Christian Vernesi. 2012. "Challenges in Global Biodiversity Conservation and Solutions that Cross Sociology, Politics, Economics and Ecology." *Biology Letters* 8(6):897-899.

Hoffman, John P. 2004. "Social and Environmental Influences on Endangered Species: A Cross-National Study." *Sociological Perspectives* 47(1):79-107.

Hoppe, Robert. 2005. "Rethinking the Science-Policy Nexus: From Knowledge Utilization and Science Technology Studies to Types of Boundary Arrangements." *Poiesis & Praxis* 3(3):199-215.

Huitema, Dave, and Esther Turnhout. 2009. "Working at the Science-Policy Interface: A Discursive Analysis of Boundary Work at the Netherlands Environmental Assessment Agency." *Environmental Politics* 18(4):576-594.

Hunter, Lori M., and Joan Brehm. 2003. "Qualitative Insight into Public Knowledge of, and Concern with, Biodiversity." *Human Ecology* 31(2): 309-320.

Hunter, Lori M., and Lesley Rinner. 2004. "The Association Between Environmental Perspective and Knowledge and Concern with Species Diversity." *Society and Natural Resources* 17:517-532.

Hunter, Lori M., Alison Hatch, and Aaron Johnson. 2004. "Cross-National Gender Variation in Environmental Behaviors." *Social Science Quarterly* 85(3):677-694.

Hunter, Lori M., Jason D. Boardman, and Jarron M. Saint Onge. 2005. "The Association Between Natural Amenities, Rural Population Growth, and Long-Term Residents' Economic Well-Being." *Rural Sociology* 70(4):452-469.

Huvila, Isto. 2011. "The Politics of Boundary Objects: Hegemonic Interventions and the Making of a Document." *JASIST* 62(12):2528-2539.

Igoe, Jim and Dan Brockington. 2007. "Neoliberal Conservation: A Brief Introduction." *Conservation & Society* 5(4):432-449.

Isaac, Larry W. 1997. "Transforming Localities: Reflections on Time, Causality, and Narrative in Contemporary Historical Sociology." *Historical Methods* 30(1): 4-12.

Jaques, Elliott. 1982. *The Form of Time.* New York, NY: Crane, Russak.

Jasanoff, Sheila. 1990. *The Fifth Branch: Science Advisors as Policymakers.* Cambridge, MA: Harvard University Press.

Johnson, Erik W. 2008. "Social Movement Size, Organizational Diversity and the Making of Federal Law." *Social Forces* 86(3):967-993.

Jones, Samantha. 2005. "Community-Based Ecotourism: The Significance of Social Capital." *Annals of Tourism Research* 32(2):303-324.

Jorgenson, Andrew K. 2006. "Unequal Ecological Exchange and Environmental Degradation: A Theoretical Proposition and Cross-national Study of Deforestation, 1990–2000." *Rural Sociology* 71(4):685-712.

Jordan, Sarah Foltz, Scott Hoffman Black, and Sarina Jepsen. 2012. "Petition to List the Island Marble Butterfly, *Euchloe ausonides insulanus* as an Endangered Species under the U.S. Endangered Species Act." The Xerces Society for Invertebrate Conservation.

Kaufman, Scott. 2004. *The Pig War: The United States, Britain, and the Balance of Power in the Pacific Northwest, 1846-72.* Lanham, MD: Lexington Books.

Kellert, Stephen R. 1985. "Social and Perceptual Factors in Endangered Species Management." *The Journal of Wildlife Management* 49(2):528-536.

Kennedy, Emily Huddart, Thomas M. Beckley, Bonita L. McFarlane, and Solange Nadeau. 2009. "Why We Don't 'Walk the Talk': Understanding the Environmental Values/Behaviour Gap in Canada." *Research in Human Ecology* 16(2):151-160.

Kennedy, Emily H., and Liz Dzialo. 2015. "Locating Gender in Environmental Sociology." *Sociology Compass* 9(10):920-929.

Kimmerer, Robin Wall. 2013. *Braiding Sweetgrass: Indigenous Wisdom, Scientific Knowledge and the Teachings of Plants.* Minneapolis, MN: Milkweed Editions.

Kirchhoff, Christine J., Maria Carmen Lemon, and Nathan L. Engle. 2013. "What Influences Climate Information Use in Water Management? The Role of Boundary Organizations and Governance Regimes in Brazil and the U.S." *Environmental Science and Policy* 26:6-18.

Kirksey, Eben. 2014. *The Multispecies Salon.* Durham, NC: Duke University Press.

Knight, Danica K., Jennifer E. Becan, and Patrick M. Flynn. 2012. "Organizational Consequences of Staff Turnover in Outpatient Substance Abuse Treatment Programs." *Journal of Substance Abuse Treatment* 42(2):143-150.

Kollmuss, Anja, and Julian Agyeman. 2002. "Mind the Gap: Why do People Act Environmentally and What Are the Barriers to Pro-Environmental Behavior?" *Environmental Education Research* 8(3):239-260.

Kümmerer, K. 1993. "'Zeiten der Natur – Zeiten des Mesnchen.'" Ein Beitrag zur Ökologie der Zeit." Pp.85-104 in *Ökologie der Zeit - Vom Finden der rechten Zeitmaße,* edited by M. Held and K. A. Geißler. Stuttgart: S. Hirzel Verlag.

Kurath, Monika Maria. 2015. "Architecture as a Science: Boundary Work and the Demarcation of Design Knowledge from Research." *Science and Technology Studies* 28(3):81-100.

Laidley, Thomas. 2013. "Climate, Class and Culture: Political Issues as Cultural Signifiers in the US." *The Sociological Review* 61(1):153-171.

Lambert, Amy Michelle. 2011. "Natural History and Population Ecology of a Rare Pierid Butterfly, *Euchloe ausonides insulanus* Guppy and Shepard (Pieridae)." (Dissertation: University of Washington).

Lamont, Michèle, and Virag Molnar. 2002. "The Study of Boundaries in the Social Sciences". *Annual Review of Sociology* 28:167–195.

Landesman, Charles, and Roblin Meeks. 2003. *Philosophical Skepticism.* Malden, MA: Blackwell Publishers, Ltd.

Langpap, Christian, and Joe Kerkvliet. 2010. "Allocating Conservation Resources Under the Endangered Species Act." *American Journal of Agricultural Economics* 92(1):110-124.

Latour, Bruno. 2005. *Reassembling the Social: An Introduction to Actor-network-theory.* Oxford, NY: Oxford University Press.

Lave, Rebecca, Philip Mirowski, and Samuel Randalls. 2010. "Introduction: STS and Neoliberal Science." *Social Studies of Science* 40(5):659-675.

Lee, Yong-ki, Sally Kim, Min-seong Kim and Jeang-gu Choi. 2014. "Antecedent and Interrelationships of Three Types of Pro-Environmental Behavior." *Journal of Business Research* 67(10):2097-2105.

Leisher, Craig, M. Sanjayan, Jill Blockhus, S. Neil Larsen, and Andreas Kontoleon. "Does Conservign Biodiversity Work to Reduce Poverty? A State of Knowledge Review." Pp. 145-159 in *Biodiversity Conservation and Poverty Alleviation: Exploring the Evidence for a Link*, edited by D. Roe, J. Elliott, C. Sandbrook, and M. Walpole. Hoboken, NJ: John Wiley & Sons.

Leonard, Madeleine. 2016. *The Sociology of Children, Childhood and Generation*. London, UK: Sage Publications Ltd.

Li, De-Zhu, and Hugh. W. Pritchard. 2009. "The Science and Economics of *Ex Situ* Plant Conservation." *Trends in Plant Science* 14(11):614-621.

Livingstone, Frank B., and Theodosius Dobzhansky. 1962. "On the Non-Existence of Human Races." *Current Anthropology* 3(3):279-281.

Lukes, Steven. 1986. *Power*. New York, NY: New York University Press.

Lukes, Steven. 2005. *Power: A Radical View*. New York, NY: Palgrave MacMillan.

Machlis, Gary E. 1992. "The contribution of sociology to biodiversity research and management." *Biological Conservation* 62:161-170.

MacLaren, Ian S. 2011. "Rejuvenating Wilderness: The Challenge of Reintegrating Aboriginal Peoples in the 'Playground' of Jasper National Park." In *A Century of Parks Canada 1911-2011*, edited by C. Campbell. Calgary, CA: Calgary University Press.

Manfredo, Michael, Tara Teel, and Alan Bright. 2003. "Why are Public Values Toward Wildlife Changing?" *Human Dimensions of Wildlife* 8(4):287-306.

Mascia, Michael B., J. Peter Brosius, Tracy A. Dobson, Bruce C. Forbes, Leah Horowitz, Margaret A. McKean, and Nancy J. Turner. 2003. "Conservation and the Social Sciences." *Conservation Biology* 17(3):649-650.

Mayer, Karl Ulrich. 2009. "New Directions in Life Course Research." *Annual Review of Sociology* 35:413-433.

McCright, Aaron M. 2010. "The Effects of Gender on Climate Change Knowledge and Concern in the American Public." *Population and Environment* 32:66-87.

McKinney, Laura A., Edward L. Kick, and Gregory M. Fulkerson. 2010. "World System, Anthropogenic, and Ecological Threats to Bird and Mammal Species: A Structural Equation Analysis of Biodiversity Loss." Organization& Environment 23(1):3-31.

McNeely, Jeffrey A. 1995. *Expanding Partnerships in Conservation*. Washington D.C.: Island Press.

Mead, George H. 1932. *The Philosophy of the Present*. Chicago, IL: Open Court Publishing Co.

Meier, Kenneth J. and Gregory C. Hill. "Bureaucracy in the Twenty-First Century." Pp. 51-71 in *The Oxford Handbook of Public Management*, edited by Ewan Ferlie, Laurence E. Lynn Jr., and Christopher Pollitt. Oxford, UK: Oxford University Press.

Meyer, John W., David John Frank, Ann Hironaka, Evan Schofer, and Nancy Brandon Tuma. 1997. "The Structuring of a World Environmental Regime, 1870-1990." *International Organization* 51(4):623-651.

Mies, Maria, and Vandana Shiva. 2014. *Ecofeminism*. London, UK: Zed Books.

Miller, Clark. 2001. "Hybrid Management: Boundary Organizations, Science Policy, and Environmental Governance in the Climate Regime." *Science, Technology, & Human Values* 26(4):478-500.

Miskelly, James W. 2000. "Habitat requirements and conservation of the butterflies Euchloe ausonides insulanus (Pieridae) and Euphydryas editha taylori (Nymphalidae) in southwestern British Columbia." Master of Science Thesis, University of Victoria.

Miskelly, James 2005. "2005 surveys for Island Marble butterfly (Euchloe ausonides insulanus) in northern coastal Washington." Washington Department of Fish and Wildlife report.

Miskelly, James, and John Fleckenstein. 2007. "Surveys for Island Marble Butterfly (Euchloe ausonides insulanus) in San Juan County, Washington, 2006." Washington Department of Natural Resources report.

Miskelly, James, and Ann Potter. 2009. "Surveys for Island Marble Butterfly (Euchloe ausonides insulanus) in San Juan County, Washington, 2007." Washington Department of Fish and Wildlife report.

Mitchell, Ronald B. 2003. "International Environmental Agreements: A Survey of Their Features, Formation, and Effects." *Annual Review of Environmental Resources* 28:429-461.

Mohai, Paul. 1985. "Public Concern and Elite Involvement in Environmental-Conservation Issues." *Social Science Quarterly* 66(4):820-838.

Mol, Arthur P.J., David A. Sonnenfeld, and Gert Spaargaren. 2009. *The Ecological Modernisation Reader: Environmental Reform in Theory and Practice.* London, UK: Routledge.

Moon, Katie, Tom D. Brewer, Stephanie R. Januchowski-Hartley, Vanessa M. Adams, and Deborah A. Blackman. 2016. "A Guideline to Improve Qualitative Social Science Publishing in Ecology and Conservation Journals." *Ecology and Society* 21(3):17.

Mortimore, Michael. 2012. "Linking Biodiversity and Poverty Alleviation in the Drylands—The Concept of 'Useful' Biodiversity." Pp. 113-126 in *Biodiversity Conservation and Poverty Alleviation: Exploring the Evidence for a Link*, edited by D. Roe, J. Elliott, C. Sandbrook, and M. Walpole. Hoboken, NJ: John Wiley & Sons.

National Park Service. 2018. "Island Marble Butterfly." Retrieved October 2, 2019 https://www.nps.gov/sajh/learn/nature/island-marble-butterfly.htm

National Park Service. 2021. "The First Ones." Retrieved July 2, 2021 https://www.nps.gov/sajh/learn/historyculture/the-first-ones.htm

Nel, Jeanne L., Dirk J. Roux, Amanda Driver, Liesl Hill, Ashton C. Maherry, Kate Snaddon, Chantel R. Petersen, Lindie B. Smith-Adao, Heidi Van Deventer, and Belinda Reyers. 2015. "Knowledge Co-Production and Boundary Work to Promote Implementation of Conservation Plans." *Conservation Biology* 30(1):176-188.

Norgaard, Kari M. 2011. *Living in Denial: Climate Change, Emotions, and Everyday Life.* Cambridge, MA: The MIT Press.

Nowotny, Helga. 1992. "Time and Social Theory: Towards a Social Theory of Time." *Time and Society* 1(3):421.

Nyland, Chris. 1990. "Capitalism and the History of Work-time Thought." Pp. 130-151 in *The Sociology of Time*, edited by John Hassard. New York, NY: St. Martin's Press.

Ojeda, Diana. 2012. "Green Pretexts: Ecotourism, Neoliberal Conservation and Land Grabbing in Tayrona National Park, Colombia." *The Journal of Peasant Studies* 39(2):357-375.

Owens, Susan, Judith Petts, and Harriet Bulkeley. 2006. "Boundary Work: Knowledge, Policy, and the Urban Environment." *Environment and Planning C: Government and Policy* 24(5):633-643.

Pailthorp, Bellamy. 2019. "Conservation Pleas to Private Landowners: Skip Red Tape and Help the Island Marble Butterfly." *KNKX*. Nov. 12, 2019. https://www.knkx.org/post/conservation-plea-private-landowners-skip-red-tape-and-help-island-marble-butterfly. Accessed February 2, 2020.

Papworth, Sarah. 2017. "Decision-Making Psychology Can Bolster Conservation." *Nature Ecology & Evolution* 1:1217-1218.

Parker, John N., and Edward J. Hackett. 2012. "Hot Spots and Hot Moments in Scientific Collaborations and Social Movements." *American Sociological Review* 77(1):21-44.

Pedersen, Helena and Vasile Stenescu. "Conclusion: Future Directions for Critical Animal Studies." Pp. 262-276 in *The Rise of Critical Animal Studies: From the Margins to the Centre*, edited by Nik Taylor and Richard Twine. New York, NY: Routledge.

Pellow, David N., and Hollie Nyseth Brehm. 2013. "An Environmental Sociology for the Twenty-First Century." *Annual Review of Sociology* 39:229-250.

Pergrams, Oliver R. W. 2019. "Conservation sociology." Retrieved October 2, 2019 (https://pergams.com/conservation-sociology).

Perlow, Leslie. 1997. *Finding Time: How Corporations, Individuals, and Families Can Benefit from New Work Practices*. Ithaca, NY: Cornell University Press.

Peterson, M. Nils, Markus J. Peterson, and Tarla Rai Peterson. 2005. "Conservation and the Myth of Consensus." *Conservation Biology* 19(3):762-767.

Peterson, M. Nils, Markus J. Peterson, and Tarla Rai Peterson. 2006. "Why Conservation Needs Dissent." *Conservation Biology* 20(2):576-578.

Peterson, M. Nils, Markus J. Peterson, Tarla Rai Peterson, and Kirsten Leong. 2013. "Why Transforming Biodiversity Conservation Conflict is Essential and How to Begin." *Pacific Conservation Biology* 19(2):94-103.

Petts, Judith and Catherine Brooks. 2006. "Expert Conceptualisations of the Role of Lay Knowledge in Environmental Decisionmaking: Challenges for Deliberative Democracy." *Environment and Planning A: Economy and Space* 38(6):1045-1059.

Pham, Thu Thuy, Bruce M. Campbell, Stephen Garnett, Heather Aslin, and Hoang Minh Ha. 2010. "Importance and Impacts of Intermediary Boundary Organizations in Facilitating Payment for Environmental Services in Vietnam." *Environmental Conservation* 37(1):64-72.

Pinchot, Gifford, and Elizabeth Pinchot. 1994. *The End of Bureaucracy & the Rise of the Intelligent Organization*. San Francisco, CA: Berrett-Koehler Publishers, Inc.

Plumwood, Val. 1993. *Feminism and the Mastery of Nature*. New York, NY: Routledge.

Postone, Moishe. 1993. *Time, Labor, and Social Domination: A Reinterpretation of Marx's Critical Theory*. Cambridge, UK: Cambridge University Press.

Potter, Ann, Thor Hanson, and Susan Vernon. 2011. "Surveys for the island marble butterfly (*Euchloe ausonides insulanus*) in San Juan County, Washington, 2010." Washington Department of Fish and Wildlife report. Olympia, Washington.

Press, Daniel, Daniel F. Doak, and Paul Steinberg. 1996. "The Role of Local Government in the Conservation of Rare Species." *Conservation Biology* 10(6): 1538-1548.

Puckett, Emily E., Dylan C. Kesler, and D. Noah Greenwald. 2016. "Taxa, Petitioning Agency, and Lawsuits Affect Time Spent Awaiting Listing Under the US Endangered Species Act." *Biological Conservation* 201:220-229.

Purcell, Kate. 2000. "Gendered Employment Insecurity?" Pp. 112-139 in *The Insecure Workforce*, edited by Edmund Heery, and John Salmon. London, UK: Rutledge.

Rabb, George B., and Carol D. Saunders. 2005. "The Future of Zoos and Aquariums: Conservation and Caring." *International Zoo Yearbook* 39(1):1-26.

Rager, A. 2001. "Die Zeit im Griff – Im Griff der Zeit. Zeitmanagement und die Suche nach einer neuen Zeitkultur." Pp.7-9 in *Wekstattbericht der Zeitakademie des Tutzinger Projekts "Ökologie der Zeit"*, edited by M. Held, and K. A. Geißler. Stuggart: S. Hirzel Verlag.

Reheis, F. 2009. "Ökologie der Zeit und politische Bildung." Online: https://www.politische-bildung-bayern.net/2009/item/173-die-oekologie-der-zeit-dr-fritz-reheis-auf-dem-netzwerkforum-2009. Accessed February 2, 2020.

Restani, Marco, and John M. Marzluff. 2002. "Funding Extinction? Biological Needs and Political Realities in the Allocation of Resources to Endangered Species Recovery: An Existing Priority System, Which Should Guide the Fish and Wildlife Service in Endangered Species Recovery, Is Ineffective, and Current Spending Patterns Decrease Long-term Viability of Island Species." *BioScience* 52(2):169-177.

Rice, James. 2007. "Ecological Unequal Exchange: Consumption, Equity, and Unsustainable Structural Relationships within the Global Economy." *International Journal of Comparative Sociology* 48(1):43-72.

Ricklefs, Robert E. 2008. *The Economy of Nature*. New York, NY: W.H. Freeman.

Robinson, Enders A. 1990. *Einstein's Relativity in Metaphor and Mathematics*. Englewood Cliffs, NJ: Prentice Hall.

Roe, Dilys, Joanna Elliott, Chris Sandbrook, and Matt Walpole. 2013. *Biodiversity Conservation and Poverty Alleviation: Exploring the Evidence for a Link*. Hoboken, NJ: John Wiley & Sons Ltd.

Rogers, Rolf E. 1969. *Max Weber's Ideal Type Theory*. New York, NY: Philosophical Library.

Rosa, Eugene A. 1999. "The Quest to Understand Society and Nature: Looking Back, but Mostly Forward." *Society & Natural Resources* 12:371-376.

Rose, David C. 2014. "The Case for Policy-Relevant Conservation Science." *Conservation Biology* 29(3):748-754.

Roth. Robin, and Wolfram Dressler. 2012. "Market-Oriented Conservation Governance: The Particularities of Place." *Geoforum* 43(3):363-366.

Royer, Ronald A., Austin, Jane E., and Wesley E. Newton. 1998. "Checklist and 'Pollard Walk' Butterfly Survey Methods on Public Lands." *The American Midland Naturalist* 140(2):358-371.

Rust, Niki A., Amber Abrams, Daniel W. S. Challender, Guillaume Chapron, Arash Ghoddousi, Jenny A. Gilkman, Catherine H. Gowan, Courtney Hughes, Archi Rastogi, Alicia Said, Alexandera Sutton, Nik Taylor, Sarah Thomas, Hita Unnikirhsnan, Amanda D. Webber, Gwen Wordingham, and Catherine M. Hill. 2017. "Quantity Does Not Always Mean Quality: The Important of Qualitative Social Science in Conservation Research." 30(10):1304-1310.

San Juan Preservation Trust. 2018. "Welcome to the World of the Island Marble Butterfly." Retrieved October 2, 2019 (https://sjpt.org/what-we-do/care-for-land/stewardship/stewardship-projects/island-marble-butterfly-project/).

Sandbrook, Chris, William M. Admas, Bram Brüscher, and Bhaska Vira. 2013. "Social Research and Biodiversity Conservation." *Conservation Biology* 27(6):1487-1490.

Sarkki, Simo, Hannu I. Heikkinen, and Riika Puhakka. 2013. "Boundary Organisations Between Conservation and Development: Insights from Oulanka National Park, Finland." *World Review of Entrepreneurship, Management and Sustainable Development* 9(1):37-63.

Saunders, Carol D. 2003. "The Emerging Field of Conservation Psychology." *Human Ecology Review* 10(2):137-149.

Saunders, Carol D., and Olin Eugene Myers Jr. 2003. "Exploring the Potential of Conservation Psychology." *Human Ecology Review* 10(2):iii-v.

Schelhas, John. 2002. "Race, Ethnicity, and Natural Resources in the United States: A Review." *Natural Resources Journal* 42(4):723-763.

Schor, Juliet. 1998. "Time, Labour and Consumption: Guest Editor's Introduction." *Time & Society* 7(1):119-127.

Schutz, Alfred. 1973. *The Structures of the Life-World.* Evanston, IL: Northwestern University Press.

Schwartz, Mark W. 2008. "The Performance of the Endangered Species Act." *Annual Review of Ecology, Evolution, and Systematics* 39:279-299.

Scoville, Caleb. 2017. "'We Need Social Scientists!' The Allure and Assumptions of Economistic Optimization in Applied Environmental Science." *Science as Culture* 26(4):468-480.

Settersten, Richard A. Jr. and Jaqueline L. Angel. 2011. *Handbook of Sociology of Aging.* New York, NY: Springer.

Shaffer, Mark L. 1981. "Minimum population sizes for species conservation." *BioScience* 31(2):131-134.

Shandra, John M., Christopher Leckband, Laura A. McKinney, and Bruce London. 2009. "Ecologically Unequal Exchange, World Polity, and Biodiversity Loss: A Cross-National Analysis of Threatened Mammals." *International Journal of Comparative Sociology* 50(3-4):285-310.

Shandra, John M., Laura A. McKinney, Christopher Leckband, and Bruce London. 2010. "Debt, Structural Adjustment, and Biodiversity Loss: A Cross-

National Analysis of Threatened Mammals and Birds." *Human Ecology Review* 17(1):18-33.

Sherman, Jennifer. 2009. *Those Who Work, Those Who Don't: Poverty, Morality, and Family in Rural America.* Minneapolis, MN: University of Minnesota Press.

Sherman, Jennifer. 2018. "'Not Allowed to Inherit My Kingdom': Amenity Development and Social Inequality in the Rural West." *Rural Sociology* 83(1):174-207.

Sherman, Jennifer. 2021. *Dividing Paradise: Rural Inequality and the Diminishing American Dream.* Oakland, CA: University of California Press.

Shogren, Jason F., John Tschirhart, Terry Anderson, Amy Whritenour Ando, Steven R. Beissinger, David Brookshire, Gardner M. Brown Jr., Don Coursey, Robert Innes, Stephen M. Meyer, and Stephen Polansky. 1999. "Why Economics Matters for Endangered Species Protection." *Conservation Biology* 13(6):1257-1261.

Shove, Elizabeth, Frank Trentmann, and Richard Wilk. 2010. *Time, Consumption and Everyday Life: Practice, Materiality and Culture.* New York, NY: Berg.

Simaika, John P., and Michael J. Samways. 2018. "Insect Conservation Psychology." *Journal of Insect Conservation* 22:635-642.

Skibins, Jeffrey C., and Robert B. Powell. 2013. "Conservation Caring: Measuring the Influence of Zoo Visitors' Connection to Wildlife on Pro-Conservation Behaviors." 32(5):528-540.

Smith, Mick. 1999. "To Speak of Trees: Social Constructivism, Environmental Values, and the Future of Deep Ecology." *Environmental Ethics* 21(4):359-376.

Smith, Rich. 2016. "All the Island Marble Butterflies on San Juan Island Might Die if Jenny Shrum and her Team Don't Save Them." *The Stranger* Dec. 6, 2016. https://www.thestranger.com/features/2016/12/06/24730138/hello-lets-talk-about-butterflies. Accessed February 2, 2020.

Sommerer, Thomas and Sijeong Lim. 2016. "The Environmental State as a Model for the World? An Analysis of Policy Repertoires in 37 Countries." *Environmental Politics* 25(1):92-115.

Sorokin, Pitirim A. and Robert K. Merton. 1937. "Social Time: A Methodological and Functional Analysis." *American Journal of Sociology* 42(5):615-629.

Sorokin, Pitirim A. 1943. *Sociocultural Causality, Space, Time: A Study of Referential Principles of Sociology and Social Science.* New York, NY: Russell & Russell.

Spencer, Martin E. 1970. "Weber on Legitimate Norms and Authority." *The British Journal of Sociology* 21:2(123-134).

Speth, James Gustave. 2014. *Angels by the River: A Memoir.* White River Junction, VT: Chelsea Green Publishing.

Star, Susan Leigh, and James R. Griesemer. 1989. "Institutional Ecology, 'Translations' and Boundary Objects: Amateurs and Professionals in Berkeley's Museum of Vertebrate Zoology, 1907-39." *Social Studies of Science* 19(3):387-420.

Stern, Paul C., Thomas Dietz, Troy D. Abel, Greg Guagnano, and Linda Kalof. 1999. "A Value-Belief-Norm Theory of Support for Social Movements: The Case of Environmentalism." *Research in Human Ecology* 6(2):81-97.

Stern, Paul C. 2000. "Toward a Coherent Theory of Environmentally-Significant Behaviour." *Journal of Social Issues* 56:407-424.

Stich, Amy E., and Julia E. Colyar. 2015. "Thinking Relationally About Studying 'Up'." *British Journal of Sociology of Education* 36(5):729-746.

Strauss, Anselm, and Juliet M. Corbin. 1997. *Grounded Theory in Practice.* Thousand Oaks, CA: Sage Publications, Inc.

Teel, Tara L., and Michael J. Manfredo. 2010. "Understanding the Diversity of Public Interests in Wildlife Conservation." *Conservation Biology* 24(1):128-139.

Thompson, E. P. 1967. "Time, Work-Discipline, and Industrial Capitalism." *Past and Present* 38:56-97.

Thrift, Nigel J. 1983. "On the Determination of Social Action in Space and Time." *Environment and Planning D: Society and Space* 1:23-57.

Tindall, D.B., Scott Davies, and Céline Mauboulès. 2003. "Activism and Conservation Behavior in an Environmental Movement: The Contradictory Effects of Gender." *Society and Natural Resources* 16:909-932.

Turner, Will R., Katrina Brandon, Thomas M. Brooks, Claude Fascon, Holly K. Gibbs, Keith Lawrence, Russell A. Mittermeir, and Elizabeth R. Selig. 2012. "The Potential, Realised and Essential Ecosystem Service Benefits of Biodiversity Conservation." Pp. 21-35 in *Biodiversity Conservation and Poverty Alleviation: Exploring the Evidence for a Link,* edited by D. Roe, J. Elliott, C. Sandbrook, and M. Walpole. Hoboken, NJ: John Wiley & Sons.

Turner, Chris. 2013. *The War on Science: Muzzled Scientists and Willful Blindness in Stephen Harper's Canada.* Vancouver, CA: Greystone Books.

Urry, John. 2016. *What is the Future?* Cambridge, UK: Polity Press.

USFWS (U.S. Fish and Wildlife Service). 2006. Endangered and threatened wildlife and plants; 12-month finding on a petition to list the island marble butterfly (*Euchloe ausonides insulanus*) as threatened or endangered. *Federal Register* 71(219):66292- 66298.

Vasseur, Michael. 2014. "Convergence and Divergence in Renewable Energy Policy Among US States from 1998 to 2011." *Social Forces* 92(4):1637-57.

Vosko, Leah F., Nancy Zukewich, and Cynthia Crawford. 2003. "Precarious Jobs: A New Typology of Employment." *Perspectives on Labour and Income* 15(4):16-26.

Wajcan, Judy. 2008. "Life in the Last Lane? Towards a Sociology of Technology and Time." *The British Journal of Sociology* 59(1):59-77.

Wittmer, Heidi, Augustin Berghöfer, and Pavan Sukhdev. 2012. "Poverty Reduction and Biodiversity Conservation: Using the Concept of Ecosystem Services to Understand the Linkages." Pp. 36-51 in *Biodiversity Conservation and Poverty Alleviation: Exploring the Evidence for a Link,* edited by D. Roe, J. Elliott, C. Sandbrook, and M. Walpole. Hoboken, NJ: John Wiley & Sons.

Wood, Alexander, Pamela Stedman-Edwards, and Johanna Mang. 2000. *The Root Causes of Biodiversity Loss.* UK: Earthscan Publications Ltd.

Wyborn, Carina. 2015. "Connectivity Conservation: Boundary Objects, Science Narratives and the Co-Production of Science and Practice." *Environmental Science and Policy* 51:292-303.

Wynne, Brian. 1996. "May the Sheep Safely Graze? A Reflexive View of the Expert-Lay Knowledge Divide." Pp. 44-83 in *Risk, Environment, and Modernity: Towards a New Ecology*, edited by Scott M. Lash, Bronislaw Szersynski, and Brian Wynne. London, UK: Sage Publications.

York, Richard, and Brett Clark. 2010. "Critical Materialism: Science, Technology, and Environmental Sustainability." *Sociological Inquiry* 80(3):475-499.

Youdelis, Megan. 2013. "The Competitive (Dis)advantages of Ecotourism in Northern Thailand." *Geoforum* 50:161-171.

Youdelis, Megan. 2016. "'They Could Take You Out for Coffee and Call It Consultation!': The Colonial Antipolitics of Indigenous Consultation in Jasper National Park." *Environment and Planning A* 48(7):1374-1392.

Youdelis, Megan. 2018. "Austerity Politics and the Post-Politicisation of Conservation Governance in Canada." *Conservation & Society* 16(3):257-267.

Zahran, Sammy, Samuel D. Brody, Himanshu Grover and Arnold Vedlitz. 2006. "Climate Change Vulnerability and Policy Support." *Society and Natural Resources* 19(9):771-789.

Zerubavel, Eviatar. 1981. *Hidden Rhythms: Schedules and Calendars in Social Life*. Chicago, IL: Chicago University Press.

Index

www.ingramcontent.com/pod-product-compliance
Lightning Source LLC
Chambersburg PA
CBHW050519280326
41932CB00014B/2380